# Last Letter to the Pebble People

# Last Letter to the Pebble People

## "Aldie Soars"

**by Virginia Hine**

*with a foreword*
*by Elisabeth Kübler-Ross*

UNITY PRESS  SANTA CRUZ

*Published by*
*Unity Press, Santa Cruz, CA 95065*
FIRST EDITION

1. Lungs — Cancer — Biography.   2. Hine, Alden Eaton
RC280.L8H56   1979     362.1'9'699409   [B]   79-11535
ISBN 0-913300-49-7

*Book Design by Craig Caughlan*
*Cover Design by John Enright*
*Typeset in Primer and Optima by Jonathan Peck*
*Manufactured in the United States of America*

1 2 3 4 5 6 7 8 9

# Contents

# Foreword

THIS IS THE STORY of a family that has been willing to share their struggles, hopes and pains, and their ultimate acceptance of the death of a most beloved family member. It is a document of the most intimate experiences of a dying man as he is beginning to learn the ultimate lesson of not only letting go, but of the meaning of unconditional love.

It is the story of a man who, like many, has followed a career, has had a good marriage and relationship with his children, and suddenly becomes aware of a malignancy that begins to alter the course of his life. His family share with us in this moving and honest book the search for medical health, the decisions the family had to make to not only use the more acceptable scientific medical approach, but new avenues to allow the patient to control his own destiny.

The *Pebble People* is a book which should open many gates. Not about the technical know-how of terminal care, but of issues that just now are beginning to emerge in our technological, scientific society where terminal communications were once labelled as hallucinations. Aldie is a beautiful example of this kind of communication. When his son asks him with whom he was talking, he answers simply and matter-of-factly, "Death, a benevolent death." And when asked if he could see God, he nodded and smiled and said, "Yes, he's right behind death." It is dialogues like this that help us understand the importance of listening to the dying patient, trying to get a glimpse of their visions, the ensuing peace, and the beautiful assistance and help that all of us are given in these final moments when the struggle is over and acceptance replaces the previous fear, resignation, or inability to let go.

Every part of Aldie was loved. There was no more shyness, no more distance, no more ugliness in this cancer-ridden body; just the beauty and love that goes beyond the comprehension of those who have not been blessed by such an experience.

Thank you, Aldie, for sharing your final weeks with us. And thank you, Pebble People, for being willing to share this experience, although totally inadequate compared to the reality of being there, it is nevertheless very moving and very beautiful. Hopefully, it will give strength to those who have the courage to try to do it but never quite knew how to go about it.

ELISABETH KÜBLER-ROSS
Easter, 1979

# Preface

*"You must needs leave so that
I may love you for your real being."*

Pir Vilayat Inayat Khan

THE PEBBLE PEOPLE are links in a far-flung network
through which the healing power of love once flowed.

The man at the center was Alden Eaton Hine. In October
of 1974, when he was fifty-four years old, he was told he had
inoperable lung cancer and something like a year of life left
to him. In January of 1976 he died. In between a miracle
occurred – death took a whole family on a journey of discovery into a dimension beyond ordinary existence. The
journey was made in three stages, each involving fewer
people, each bringing increasing exaltation and deeper
pain. This book is dedicated to those many who accompanied us on the first stage of the journey. We called them
'Pebble People'. Together we discovered the power of love
to unite people in the face of one of life's greatest chal-
lenges, freeing them from the debilitating sense of helplessness. We came to believe in our hearts what we had only
accepted in our minds before – that mind and body are not
separate and that conventional medical therapies can be
miraculously potentiated by a determined effort to focus

non-physical powers. Our faith in the power of love was painfully tested. It took fifteen months for us to realize that there is a miracle greater than healing, a goal greater than life.

For us, to whom death was coming in the middle years, the only way to learn its majesty was to struggle against it in every way we could imagine. Some of our efforts were heroic, some absurd, laughable. But we had to be certain that this was the right time for death and that it was the right kind of death. With that certainty, Aldie was able eventually to recognize, accept, and participate actively in his dying process and to draw his close people into the miracle with him.

Perhaps the most astonishing thing we learned by participating in the death of Alden Hine was that he was not a 'victim' either of cancer or of death. He led us through the final stages of a process over which he had a remarkable degree of control. Death didn't just 'come'. Aldie worked at it, and the moment of death was his victory—and ours. I now know that those surrounding a dying person can create conditions that facilitate rather than hinder this mysterious task. A victorious death is probably as much the responsibility, and privilege, of those who love the dying person as it is of the person who is joining with his death.

This book is written as my letter to those Pebble People who joined us in the first stages of the journey but who heard of the final victory only indirectly. It is also written to anyone who is dying, to those surrounding a dying person, and to those concerned with the way of death in our society. May it enable all of us to embark upon a journey more important than the conquest of disease—the conquest of the fear of death. And may we experience the transformative power that this releases into life.

The Pebble People whose names appear in this account are listed on the following page in case, as in a Russian novel, they become confusing.

| | |
|---|---|
| JENNIFER | our sixteen-year-old daughter |
| CONNIE | our college-student daughter |
| JULIE | our oldest daughter |
| JOE | Julie's husband |
| TIP | our oldest (bachelor) son |
| RIC | our second son |
| MOLLI | Ric's wife |
| CHARLIE SEAN | Ric and Molli's sons |
| TIM | Aldie's son, my stepson |
| RICHARD CLAUDIA | close Pebble friends, now non-kin family |
| PAT | non-kin family, living in the greenhouse |
| MATT | Jennifer's friend |
| MERDI | Aldie's daughter, my stepdaughter |
| SUZIE | non-kin "daughter," lived with us during her teens |
| SUZANNA | non-kin family, lives in attached apartment |
| ED | Aldie's brother |
| JANE | Ed's wife |
| MARNY | my sister |
| CHARLOTTE | Marny's friend |
| STEVE | Merdi's beloved person |
| CLYDE | Connie's beloved person |
| PETER & JOANNE | non-kin family, lived in the greenhouse for two years |

# The Training

"... both animal and man were charged by life
to do everything in their power to defeat death,
if only to make certain that when it ultimately comes
it is the right kind of death."

Laurens van der Post

# The Pebble People

FOR SOME PEOPLE a victorious death seems to occur gratu-itously. It just happens that way. I have always believed that people die in a manner consistent with the deeper levels of their life patterns. So for these fortunate souls, perhaps the whole of life is lived as an unintentional training for the good death. But for other people, like Alden Hine, a victori-ous death seems to require an intense period of very inten-tional training. They say more people are taking longer to die nowadays, thanks to our advanced technologies. Per-haps this is offering us the added time we need to learn how to die lovingly and victoriously. It would make sense. In a culture permeated by death-avoidance, people have to learn quickly, near the end, what they have rejected or been denied in a lifetime of learning.

The story of our training should probably start at the moment we realized that death was coming. It is difficult to pinpoint the moment of recognition because this kind of knowing occurs at many different levels of consciousness. Did we know with certainty that Aldie was going to die only two weeks before when he made his conscious decision to terminate all therapies and we focused our mental energies on a 'quick release'? Or was it two weeks before that, when we wept and held each other knowing we had to come to grips with surrender, and Aldie spoke of 'husband-and-wife surgery'? Or did we really know at the last family reunion in August when he sat holding his aching arm and watched the rest of us play wildly disorganized three-generation touch football? It was that night when he said suddenly in the kitchen while he was making the salad, "I realized this afternoon that I am going to die." Yet we kept on trying even after that—more radiation to knock back the tumors; more soul-searching to find what we believed to be the emotional and psychic roots of the disease.

Perhaps Aldie really knew at the beginning of our fifteen-month trial. He had experienced a series of cluster head-aches during September of 1974 which had masked the symptoms of cancer. The headaches were finally brought under control by an antihistamine program, but a weari-ness and an unexplained malaise continued. One night he said very simply, but with quiet certainty, "Bujie, I've got lung cancer. I'm going to call Ken Swords tomorrow and make an appointment for an X ray." I sat there across the counter top from him—we were having drinks before dinner—and thought, "Of course." It was a shock. But not the shock of surprise. It was the shock of recognition. Even then I wondered why I wasn't surprised.

I suspect, though, we could go even farther back than that, to a night two years before. Another night while sitting and talking over drinks at the same counter (such rivers of intimacy and communication flowed across that counter, evening after evening, year after year!), he spoke with the same quiet certainty, but this time there was energy and strength in his voice. He said that a knowledge had been stirring in the back of his mind and had just come clear that day at the marine lab.

"I think the time has come for me to wind up this era of my life," he said.

We were both excited and talked late that night. He made a long list of articles he intended to publish and research projects he wanted to complete. We thought he was going to wind up an era of his professional life and go on to some-thing else. He had made a major mid-life career change before, and we thought this was another. Only much, much later did we realize the magnitude and the nature of that 'something else'.

He never got around to most of the projects on his list. At some level he must have known, even then, that his professional life was not the focus of this change. In the very depths of our common being I think we began to prepare then for a change of much greater proportions – adjusting slowly, altering course, loving each other in subtle new ways we did not even understand, moving toward the climax of the final transformation.

Looking back over the fifteen months of our struggle with cancer, I see a rather heroic array of attempts to slow or reverse the process of the disease. All the time, through peaks of hope and valleys of despair, we were being trained, or were training ourselves, for the victorious death. Of course, we didn't recognize this until near the end. Part of the training is the hope that keeps you exquisitely poised between the realities of life and death. There are some things that you can learn only by hanging there, not knowing which way it is going to go.

We had three things going for us right at the beginning which, judging from what I have heard and read about others, were a leg up on the task we had before us. One was an openness of communication that was the product of twenty years of hard work, of painful self-revealing, and of a determination to be utterly close in the farthest recesses of our hearts and minds. Of course we often fell short of total intimacy. There were areas in each of us that we did not even know ourselves; and there were terribly painful times of separateness when the intimacy could not be sustained. But in a way, those were the little deaths that helped prepare us for the big one. One night during that first dreadful week when Aldie was in the hospital for the biopsies, I was assailed by the total horror of what death could mean and I felt that pain in the chest so familiar to any grieving person. I thought then, "Well, hello, friend. You are not such a stranger after all. I know you." Even though we often failed, openness of communication was a central tenet of our faith in love, and it helped us to avoid the incredible pretending which so many families suffer from. For some families, the training includes learning how not to pretend. That must be a difficult thing to unlearn in the shadow of death. What regrets there must be at the end of a lifetime of pretense!

The second thing we had going for us was that we never, either of us, had to suffer the very special torments of the "Why me? Why did this have to happen to me?" Somehow Aldie and I always knew "Why us?" though we had different ways of verbalizing it, depending upon the therapy we were engaged in at the time or the spiritual or mental discipline we were trying on for size. It would be nice to say that our backgrounds in science (marine biology for Aldie and anthropology for me) trained us to assume a satisfying reason for things. Ideally a scientific turn of mind should provide one with an undergirding of faith, not only in causes but in purpose. Unfortunately the opposite seems to be true. The underlying sense of purpose came from somewhere else, somewhere way back in our lives before we even met. Once we met we had a word for that purpose—"love." People who face death believing in a universe run on a rewards-and-punishment basis or a universe operating according to laws of chance and probability are going to have to resolve the crucial "Why me?" question somehow. It can be resolved. Many have done it. But for us, right from the beginning there was a reason, even a purpose, in the cancer, and it had to do with our 'usness'—with our love, the relationship that was the central fact of our lives. Later we came to talk of the cancer as something that was as much a product of our relationship as our children were. Aldie even spoke of carrying the cancer in his body for both of us as I had carried our child in my body. This made the doctors and various other therapists wince or look as if they wanted to throw up, but we didn't care. It's how it felt to us and it strengthened us in those times when stress and fear tended to drive a wedge between us. We were never able to verbalize just how the cancer was an expression of our relationship.

There was no sense of its being the result of something *wrong* or of some psychological hang ups that needed undoing or resolving. It was more an awareness of the cancer as it cut across the established patterns of our love and pushed us to some further expression of it.

The third blessing we brought to the experience from our life together was an awareness of rhythms – psychic rhythms if you will. Growth is a process of death and resurrection, of alternating waves of fear and faith, confidence and terror. The process of dying and the process of grief are growth times, times of radical transformation. Academically we talk about growth as happening in 'stages'. We then fuzz this image by saying that the stages are not 'clear cut' and can 'overlap'. Experientially, growth is far more like being at sea in gale-force winds in a rubber dinghy. Talk of progressing toward some psychological or emotional landfall is irrelevant. All you know are the incessant rhythms of up and down, swirl and churn. One moment you are in the troughs of absolute panic, seeing only thunderous destruction on all sides. The next moment you are riding the crest of hope and joy that stretches to the horizons of life and beyond.

Our life together had taught us to accept the *fact* of these rhythms, though we never accepted their troughs gracefully. My way, as we were pitching down into one of them, was to lose sight of the next crest, to agonize over the loss of the last one, and always, always to try to 'fix up' what had gone wrong. Aldie had a way of withdrawing slightly so that he was not experiencing the trough completely, waiting to unfold his sensitivity and his responsiveness until we reached the next crest. The result, of course, was that I would exert pressure on Aldie to change something which he was refusing to even experience. The crests always came again – but not because I ever 'fixed' anything. They came because we needed closeness more than we cared about what had separated us. These conflicting response patterns were to plague us cruelly during our final trial, but this too was part of the training. At the end they were resolved in the total understanding that can come with the transformation of death.

Even with our conflicting responses to the troughs, our mutual acceptance of the rhythms helped greatly. Perhaps we were freer to move more quickly through the rhythmic swings, facilitating growth. In any case, the rhythms characterized our whole fifteen months, beginning the very first day.

Aldie went to Kenneth Swords, our family doctor, the day after he announced he had lung cancer, and saw the X ray with the right lung full of white blobs and lacework. He drove home so hunched over that he was looking at the road from under the curve of the steering wheel. 'Abject terror' was the phrase he used to describe how he felt. Within the hour, though, he walked into the house clear-eyed and said with quiet assurance, "Well Bujie, we've been through a lot together and now we've got another big one coming up."

I swiveled my chair away from the desk where I'd been preparing lecture notes and watched him as he crossed the room and sat down in the armchair and looked at me. I was struck by the straightness of his back and by the intensity of the blue of his eyes. These were the signs of Aldie at his strongest, most competent best. We sat looking at each other straight on as he told me what Ken had said. It was as if at some deep level we were mobilizing, merging in a curious way, being welded into a single fighting instrument. We were not touching, nor did either of us have a need to. The 'us-ness' at that moment was quite independent of our physical bodies. Oddly enough it was even independent of what we were talking about – the facts of the disease, the approaching biopsies, and the hospital arrangements. It was as if the cancer and everything connected with it were merely the outside trappings of the real challenge that lay at the heart of it. To that challenge we brought what we had – open communication, a knowledge that love is the purpose of life, and an acceptance of the psychic rhythms that would lift us to the heights and throw us into the depths.

By the end of that week we had learned that the cancer was inoperable because it was growing on the windpipe, that it had not metastasized to other organs, and that the recommended therapy was five weeks of cobalt radiation of the right lung. We were also told that the prognosis was six months to a year *if* the radiation was successful. We were very grateful to Kenneth for telling us flat out what he had learned from the specialists and what he believed, based on his experience.

It has always seemed inconceivable to me that anyone would want less than the whole truth from a doctor. To my way of thinking, physicians are trained specialists. Some of them are very good counselors, but they are not high priests qualified to carve the truth up into digestible portions. Nor are they, as a group, especially talented guides to people facing issues of life and death. A doctor to trust is one like Kenneth Swords who will tell you whatever he knows, respect your decisions, and use his skills as best he can in facilitating your efforts to live well or to die well. Aldie and I never shared the popular assumption that in order to hold out hope a doctor must be vague about life expectancy. We knew there was no such thing as accuracy in these predictions, but we wanted to know the statistical averages for what they were worth. Our hope did not come from uncertainty, but from a known 'worst' against which we could spring into action. It put us in an active role. It also gave us a chance at that small, but surprisingly satisfying, goal for a cancer patient, 'outliving your sentence'.

We went into that first week of diagnostic tests in the hospital riding one of our crests of courage and came out crawling, our confidence battered and many of the familiar signposts of our lives torn down. They did three biopsies in two days, each more traumatic than the last. The surgeon explained it all to me before Aldie went in for the final operation in which they literally slit his throat and went down into his lung with their little bag of tools to dig out a reluctant specimen. I listened to his explanation on the phone, standing by the central nurses' desk with my finger in my other ear to keep out the noise. Why couldn't he have called me on the phone in Aldie's room? Or even more importantly, why couldn't he have explained it all directly to Aldie? He told me that the thorough series of X rays they had taken the first day had made the diagnosis clear and had also provided the information that the radiologist would need in order to direct the cobalt beams at the appropriate spots. The purpose of the final operation was not diagnostic, but to document the diagnosis with actual proof that there were demonstrably malignant cancer cells – proof without which the radiologist would refuse to treat a patient.

All of this made perfect sense to me at the time. Now, in retrospect, I realize that it didn't make any sense at all. It is absurd to make a sick person sicker by an operation that isn't going to tell you anything more than what you already know.

Through the operation we found out that Aldie's cancer was made of 'oat-cells' which respond well to radiation, but we could have found that out during radiation. We also found out that it was one of the few kinds of lung cancer that is not related to smoking, but this was irrelevant to us as we had already quit smoking. They protected us or perhaps themselves from the outside chance that the blobs on the X rays were not really cancer. But Aldie already knew it was cancer before he even made the appointment with Ken. Of course, that kind of knowing cannot be taken into account. It does not fit into the conventional framework we use to define reality.

After the final operation, Kenneth was the one to convey the information about the prognosis – out in the hall, of course, where it seems the really crucial physician-survivor conferences usually happen! I told Aldie as soon as he returned from wherever anaesthetics take you. Not surprisingly, this was about cocktail time. (We were magnificent Pavlovian specimens of our dominant culture pattern, Aldie and I. We salivated promptly at five every afternoon.) He had just gotten about half way through the first scotch and water when I repeated the prognosis. Immediately he grabbed a little half-moon plastic bowl and threw up into it. As soon as he had finished that he handed me his glass and croaked, "Fix me a drink." I resisted the rational temptation of assuming that the scotch had made him sick, and we settled down to digest both the information and more scotch, which by then was going down very suitably.

We had to decide what we thought about the suggested therapy. We understood what we could expect from conventional medical therapies and this boiled down to a game of time. With Aldie's diagnosis, talking about a 'cure' was considered naive. Even the word 'remission' made the hospital staff look uncomfortable. Medical personnel, however, did batter us endlessly with the information that "a whole lot depends on your attitude." Unfortunately they seemed helpless to say just what attitude makes which difference and, more importantly, how you go about acquiring the right attitude. This, we realized as we talked, we would have to discover for ourselves.

At one point that first week, we discussed the possibility of turning our backs on all conventional therapies with their destructive side effects and their definition of success as simply life-extension, and putting all our energies into non-medical, non-physical healing alternatives. 'Faith healing,' 'psychic healing' – these are the old-fashioned phrases that are held in such contempt in reputable circles. Newer phrases are coming into fashion now – 'holistic medicine' and 'parapsychology' seem to be more acceptable ways of mentioning the power of consciousness. Whatever the label, Aldie and I knew that there are energies that can affect the physical body in ways that are completely unexplainable using conventional medical concepts. Neither of us doubted that this path is possible for some people. We had, before and since, met and talked with people who had mind-boggling experiences that resulted in complete and well-documented remissions.

However, it did not take us long to realize that we could not in all conscience take this route to the exclusion of conventional therapies. We could not wholeheartedly subscribe to any of the belief systems inherent in non-physical alternatives. Whatever the proponents say about that not mattering, it did to us. We knew we would have to carve out our own peculiar combination of medical therapies and other approaches to healing, and that it would take some tugging and hauling. We were painfully aware that the basic assumptions underlying Western medicine are hopelessly at odds with the assumptions basic to most non-medical alternatives, and that walking with one foot in each world is not nearly as easy as some people think it is.

"It has always been our lot to bridge gaps," Aldie said during one of our hospital talks. "There's no reason why we should abandon our way now." So we decided to go along with the radiation and explore other ways too.

There was one advantage in having at least toyed with the idea of rejecting conventional therapies entirely. It freed us from one of the worst curses of the cancer sub-culture—the mad dash from one specialist to another. Those who perceive cancer as a wholly physiological, organic phenomenon are condemned to a desperate search among a bewildering array of wholly physiological 'cures' and 'breakthroughs'. Neither of us felt the slightest need to scramble around for other doctors to check out the diagnosis or suggest other treatments.

When Aldie left the hospital, his face and neck were incredibly puffed because the cancer was interfering with normal lymph system flow. He had a three-inch sausage across his throat embroidered in cross-stitch, but he felt well enough to drive the car home. It looked as if we were going to start our fight from point zero. That week after the hospital and before the radiation treatments began was

VIRGINIA HINE

a steady downhill grind. Aldie got sicker and sicker. There
were fainting spells and frightening falls, and coughing
fits that ended in momentary blackouts. He said that during
these times he felt that he was hanging between darkness
and the light—between death and life—and that it required
a tremendous effort to choose the light. Sometimes he said
he had to force himself to open his eyes because it would
have been so much easier to just sink into the dark. What we
did not find out until two months later, from a re-reading
of some postoperative X rays, was that Aldie was suffering
from an undiagnosed case of pneumonia after he left the
hospital. It made him sick enough to undermine his will
to live. I could feel him slipping away into passivity, not
caring, losing the initiative.

In the middle of one sleepless night that week we were
talking with Jennifer over a cup of boullion. Jennifer was
sixteen then, our youngest. She had carried the burden of
shock with us, and shared the enervating phone calls to
four other sons and daughters who live in other parts of
the country. We were trying to regroup, to find a handle on
what had happened to us. It occurred to me to ask Aldie
about a feeling he had expressed several times in the past
two years or so—the feeling that he had a tremendous
amount of energy that was simply not being used up by
the life he was living. We had done our best to imagine what
sorts of changes we could make that would utilize this
energy but had never been able to come up with any really
motivating thoughts. It seemed an appropriate time to take
another crack at it.

"What would happen if you were to let all of that stored
up energy inside you loose?" I asked.

"I'd have to get out of the way!"

His immediate answer seemed to surprise Aldie as much
as it did me.

"What do you mean?"

"I don't know."

"It sounds as if you're saying you'd have to die."

"No!" he said. "I don't want to die. I still have songs to sing and dreams to dream."

The words were right, so like Aldie, but Jennifer and I felt our hearts sink. The energy that belonged behind the words just wasn't there.

So Aldie embarked upon his fifteen-months' struggle from some point way below zero. As we looked back upon those first days from the vantage point of the changes that were wrought in us, we realized that at the beginning he was not so much motivated to live as he was afraid of dying. But it was enough. Those around him were highly motivated to *make* him want to live, offering him ideas and alternatives to which he could respond. It would be easy to see our whole fifteen months of life-saving efforts as an elaborate denial mechanism. Ironically, some of these attempts were absolutely essential to the victorious death that crowned our efforts.

The first of our attempts to halt or reverse the process of the disease was one we created ourselves; one that was a direct outgrowth of our particular life-style and the kind of love to which we had committed ourselves years earlier.

Aldie and I believed that when two people commit themselves wholly to each other, in the same way that truly religious people give themselves over to God, they gain access to a transforming power. At the beginning of our life together, there were religious people who told us our ideas were sacrilegious. We were putting another human being above God. There were also psychologists who said we were unhealthily dependent upon each other. But none of our critics seemed to have as much love bubbling up unhindered from the wellsprings of their lives. So, we followed where the love led, formulating what we believed as we went along. Aldie wrote in a letter during our early days:

> Can unmotivated, spontaneous love originate from other than a state of oneness, where oneness is fulfillment in itself, seeking aught else?

Admittedly it was hard to maintain this under the pressure of daily life. Total self-giving requires a defenselessness, a willingness to be wholly vulnerable, a patience with one's own inadequacies. Total acceptance requires access to that divine state above dualities where one can truly say, "it doesn't matter," where the response to injury is loving sadness rather than anger. Aldie and I found ways to keep the wellspring clear most of the time in dealing with our children and others. In the magic circle of our closeness nothing else mattered. We could blot up, absorb, and eliminate the natural angers inspired by others, and remove the burden of expectancies from our love for the children. When love does not demand a particular return, it enhances, freeing people for self-creation. It was between the two of us where we most often fell short of our dream. What we could do for others we often failed to do for each other, because it was precisely *from* each other that we most desperately needed a return. The pressure of total self-giving was sometimes more than Aldie could cope with, given his particular background and personality. His escape was through temporary withdrawals (usually drinking too much) and through a remarkable ability – which he realized with a shock later in our fifteen months – to simply block the memory of anger-withdrawals out of his mind. On the other hand, my fatal flaw was the inability to hang on to "it doesn't matter." I could not, no matter how hard I tried, accept his withdrawing self. I would feel anger, which took the form of a gray film cast over our lives. We went to a psychiatrist once for help in breaking through this mutual downward-spiral pattern, and he tried to get us to express our angers. So we yelled and threw clocks for a while, but that wasn't the answer at all. We found that it does no good to express anger at someone for something that person cannot change. You simply have to die inside and wait until the oneness surges back of its own accord. It will, although you can never believe it no matter how many times you've been through it.

During the separate times, we could be just as loving and responsive to others and, in terms of practical daily life, to each other. But inside, it was like two people standing on opposite sides of a canyon yearning to touch fingertips. In the end the essential oneness always reasserted itself, making withdrawal unnecessary and washing away the anger. Even though our lives seemed to be a series of little deaths and resurrections, the transforming quality of our commitment to total self-giving and total acceptance seemed to keep on working. We began to notice it spill over, changing people who lived in that atmosphere even for a few weeks or months.

By the time of the diagnosis we had a large network of people who had lived with us over the years—more than we could count. We had our own five children, now grown—four of them my natural children whom Aldie adopted and one of our own. In addition, children from Aldie's former marriage were our good friends and sometimes brief residents in our home. The rest were what we called our non-biological kin. Some of these needed a home for a week or two, some for a couple of years. Some were wounded birds, friends of our own children who for one reason or another were denied their own homes. Later there were members of the 'counterculture' who joined us in exploring the possibilities of the new kind of extended-family living.

As people flowed through this house and moved on in the world, a network of love began to connect us to many people in far places. Even though they no longer lived with us, the transforming quality of the love seemed to linger on. None of us were quite the same after the time of living together. Each relationship added a different dimension to Aldie's and my experience, as our particular adequacies and inadequacies, given in love, seemed to alter the course of their lives. So we knew the power of love to change things. From this concept of love and from the network of people who had shared it with us, came our first attempt to participate in and affect the disease process.

The idea was born at the same blessed counter during the week after the biopsies and before the radiation therapy had started. Our daughter Connie had come from California to help get the neglected house back on an even keel and we were watching her make dinner. We were talking about the expressions of concern that had begun to flow in our direction as news of the diagnosis was communicated to family and to people with whom professional engagements had to be cancelled. Always the question was, "What can I do to help?" invariably spoken in a tone that conveyed such helplessness. In truth, our answer at that point had to be, "Nothing much," no matter how gently we phrased it. We are not the kind of family that can easily say, "Pray for us," for to too many people in our love network the word 'pray' does not signify a meaningful nor effective kind of activity. It would have sounded more like a pious turn-off.

We had no quarrel with those who preached the power of God to heal. It was just that we didn't believe it would work for us as it does for them. We had seen it happen, but it always seemed to be within the context of a strongly committed and believing group. We had never been able to give ourselves completely to the belief systems of such groups, for our experience of how to love didn't seem to fit.

As Aldie and Connie and I talked that night, we realized that we did have something that everyone in our close relationship network recognized as a source of strength and power. All of us believed in the power of love as we had experienced it to change the direction of a life. I believed that this power could also affect physiological processes taking place in Aldie's body. Not that it would, but that it *could*. There is a difference. Aldie *wanted* to believe. That is about all he could do with the misery in his body sapping away at his will to live. So Connie and I believed for him. The three of us started to talk about the possibility of focusing all that love that had been building up all of those years. We decided to ask the people who had said, "What can I do?" to take ten or fifteen minutes every day and just concentrate on Aldie. We really believed in what I would now call the power of consensus. We had no words for it then. We just knew that when people join their energy streams miracles happen. Rituals are formalized ways of joining energy streams. Traditional rituals didn't work for us, so we tried creating one of our own.

It came to be called the Pebble People network.

We thought that if everyone who loved Aldie could focus his or her thought-energy on the idea of healing at the same time of day, we could tap a source of energy that is available, but must be harnessed. We imagined this energy source to be like the rays of the sun which warm the earth but will not start a fire unless you use the old Boy Scout magnifying glass trick on dry leaves.

Five o'clock seemed the logical time of day, because like most people, it had always marked our shift from focus out into the world to focus in on the enjoyment of each other. The cocktail hour was our ritual, and we saw nothing wrong with juxtaposing two types of rituals. As we talked, the wording of a letter began to form. We decided not to use the phraseology of any traditional religious belief because it seemed to muddy things up for so many people these days. It was Connie who added the idea about the pebbles. She thought people needed a concrete symbol of their commitment to our healing experiment. About fifty copies of this letter were mailed the next day to our network—biological family, non-kin family, close friends, and a few concerned professional colleagues. It included a 'Statement of Hope'.

> WE KNOW that the cancer can be reduced in size and its malignant spread slowed down, extending the period of life for several months.
>
> WE HOPE that the cancer will be removed completely and that Aldie will live many years in full and active health.
>
> WE BELIEVE that energy forces for healing, beyond present

medical knowledge, exist and can be tapped if many people join their thoughts and love together for this purpose. We think that the power of focused love can 'irradiate' the body in cooperation with the cobalt beam, helping to break up the cancer cells and providing a protective shield preventing damage to healthy cells.

WE PROPOSE to organize ourselves to tap the healing energy-force by coming together each day at 5:00 PM for ten or fifteen minutes by ourselves or with anyone who is moved to come here at this time. In silence we will concentrate our love and thoughts on these ideas and hopes. We will begin on November 11, the first day of the cobalt treatments, and continue until the treatments are completed. That date will be communicated through the network.

WE ASK anyone, anywhere, who wants to join us in thought to do the same thing, perhaps at the same time of day if this is fitting. We will be sitting near a little fountain lined with stones which we built together during the last two months. We recognize the power of symbolic acts and objects. We have each put a pebble in the lower pool to remind us daily of our commitment to a power beyond ourselves. We ask that anyone who wants to join us in our faith in life send us a pebble or small stone from some place you have loved. Each day at the joining time, Aldie will put into the pool any pebbles that have come, and the name of its sender will be in our hearts with gratitude. Each pebble will be to us a symbol of the love and concern people have expressed for us, and we know already how strengthening this has been.

The response to our statement of hope was really remarkable. It was as if we had struck a chord that resonated with a new kind of hope already in people's minds, waiting to be put to work. The first day, twenty people arrived at our doorstep each bearing a pebble! We couldn't believe it. No one knew how to act. Aldie couldn't decide whether to play the part of host or ritual leader. In the end we all sort of straggled out to the terrace where the fountain was and arranged ourselves on flagstones and rocks while Aldie crouched by the pool, placing each pebble carefully into the water.

Aldie was still very sick the day the radiation began. He said that as he knelt there by the pool that evening, he felt an incredible thrust, almost like a physical force, coming from the people gathered behind him. Twice during that first week he felt a "shimmering sensation," like electricity, running the length of his body. After that first day there were always eight or ten people gathered at five — some regulars, many occasional drop-ins.

Then the pebbles started to come through the mail from other parts of the country, each with a little story about where the pebble came from and why it was meaningful to its sender. The network began to grow. Friends of friends of friends sent pebbles and even thanked us for the opportunity to share in our experience. Some people prayed, some meditated, some concentrated, and some just sat outside and looked at trees and thought about Aldie. By the time we sent out the last letter to the Pebble People network, our mailings were going to over two hundred people. Even our friend the postman, whose curiosity about the lumpy letters we were receiving brought him into the network, left us three pebbles in the mailbox one day with a note saying, "For faith, for hope, and for love."

As is usual in a life crisis, people we knew very superficially rose to do battle beside us, and strong new bonds were formed. Claudia and Richard, who were to play major roles in the victorious death, were two of these. The night of Aldie's visit to Ken for the very first X ray, was Richard's thirty-seventh birthday and we had planned a special dinner together. Not wanting to disappoint them, and not feeling that we were close enough to share our shock with them, we thought we could make it through dinner-as-usual. Before the meal even came, we realized we couldn't and told them why we appeared so distracted. The shock silenced them. After one or two fumbling questions and equally fumbling answers, the subject was dropped. We thought they were people who just couldn't handle the terrible immediacy of death in the context of an undemanding social relationship. How wrong we were. They simply needed time to digest the unexpected information. They appeared at five o'clock that first day of the network and never quit. Their determined support all through the fifteen months drew them into the intimate circle of our non-kin family household.

The five-week radiation program was marvelously successful. The radiologists were surprised at the rate of tumor-reduction and at the complete lack of side effects, but they were acutely uncomfortable when we made the mistake of mentioning the network activities. They averted their eyes with a combination of pity and contempt. They seemed to have forgotten that they had told us that "a lot depends on your attitude." At the very least we had discovered a mechanism by which to create a 'positive attitude'. As Aldie said later, the network provided him with the will to live when he had lost it. "I couldn't die. The whole group was counting on me!" Of course, we believed that the network did much more than that, and so did the two-hundred-odd Pebble People. Call it the power of an attitude, call it the power of love, call it the power of God – we did have our miracle. Its development is recorded in the letters we sent to the Pebble People during the next two months:

Dearly Beloved Pebble People:
It has been just over a month since we started to meet with you in thought, in spirit, and in love. We said then that we *believed* there are energy-forces for healing that could be tapped if many people joined their love and thoughts together for this purpose. Now we *know* that this is true.

The changes in the last month have been dramatic. The cancer has been reduced more quickly and to a smaller size than was originally hoped and Aldie has had NO side effects – the 'radiation sickness' you see and hear so much of in the radiologists' waiting rooms! People who have joined us here by the fountain for the five o'clock quiet time have seen the transformation.

On November 11th, when the cobalt treatments started and you began to send your energies flowing through the network, Aldie was very weak, had little appetite, slept badly and only in a reclining chair because he couldn't lie down flat. Coughing was severe and involved panicky moments of not being able to breathe. His face and arms were swollen because of the cancer pressure and lymph node enlargement.

During the second week the changes began. Just when the radiologists said he might begin to feel the effect of the radiation, all his symptoms disappeared. He began to eat normally. He started going for long walks, did all the driving, hauled wood for the fire, paid bills and all those uglies, and began to make his usual whimsies. The swelling in his face and neck went down, the lymph nodes under his arms and in his neck shrank to normal size. He was able to sleep all night in bed, even on his right side, and by the end of the third week the coughing was much better.

As with any journey into joy and faith, the path has led both up and down. There are very few plateaus—mostly peaks and valleys. Faith alternates with fear, hope with doubt, in a ceaseless and creative rhythm. Our ups are really high! Life sparkles with new light, the simplest things are beautiful. At such times our hearts fairly explode with gratitude for the network. For the energizing certainty that lifts us into health of mind and body could never be generated or sustained for long by the two of us alone.

The downs are frightening, of course, because doubt and fear lead quite literally to death. It is too easy to let conventional assumptions creep in—assumptions that equate cancer with death and limit hope to a period of 'remission'. Then the future darkens and seems full of pain. We have seen the eyes of people at the radiation center who take these things for granted. They have given up inside and death walks with them. It is sad, but some of the doctors are our worst enemies. It takes strength beyond what we two can muster to fight off the unspoken negativism. That strength comes from all of you. When we feel ourselves sliding down into the abyss, we have but to look at the pebbles in the pool—each with its own story and its special meaning—and we know we are safe. Like any node in any network, we can only slide so far before we feel the linkages, extending out in space and time, pulling us back up.

By Christmas week the cobalt treatments should be over. It seems we Pebble People are not alone in our conviction that the outcome need not be left to 'chance.' Thanks to

several people in the Pebble network we have made contact
with two centers where reputable people are researching
the healing power of certain thought modes. One is in
Texas, the other California. We hope to visit them both
in January.

Whatever we learn from these people, we know we must
go on with our daily joining-in-the-spirit time as a way of
keeping ourselves focused on that which gives life in the
midst of death, faith in the midst of fear, peace in the
struggle, and love above all! Bless hearts all!

Of the dozens of suggestions about new approaches to
cancer that were coming in through the network, Aldie
had chosen one that appealed to him the most. It was the
work of Dr. O. Carl Simonton, a cancer specialist in Fort
Worth who combined conventional therapies with a program of meditation based on the demonstrable power of
visualizations and mental imagery to affect physiological
processes. It was during our first visit to investigate Dr.
Simonton's program, that we learned of the remarkable
changes that had occurred between the termination of
radiation treatments in mid-December and the visit to
Fort Worth in mid-January, when new X rays were taken.
While the effects of radiation often continue for a time
after the treatment stops, it is impossible not to believe
that the continuing energy input from the network during
that month had had its effect also. By the time of the Fort
Worth trip, Aldie felt that we had discovered the next step
in our journey toward life, and he wrote the second letter
to the Pebble People:

Dearly Beloved Pebble People:

We have just returned from Fort Worth, Texas, where we
spent five days with Dr. Carl Simonton, five other 'terminal'
cancer patients, and the patients' spouses. I've seldom
seen a healthier looking group of people! Dr. Simonton
believes that the human body is able to activate or reinforce
its own immune system through meditation and specially
designed visualizations, and we feel that this is the direction in which we now want to go. While we were there, we
discovered two things that should be of interest to all of
you who have worked so hard.

On October 25th, when the cancer was diagnosed, the primary tumor was the size of your fist and was located in the upper tracheal region. A smaller metastatic tumor was located near the periphery of the same lung. At the end of the cobalt treatments the primary tumor was reduced 50% in size and the metastatic tumor about 25%. Since then the only 'treatment' I have received has come from all of you. The X rays taken last week in Fort Worth showed the primary tumor to be now a 1 cm encysted node. The secondary tumor has disappeared, and the spaces originally occupied by both have regenerated normal healthy lung tissue, with the exception of some scar tissue near the site of the original secondary tumor.

A critical part of this life experience occurred in November although we did not know it at the time. Only a recent review of the X rays showed a dangerous case of pneumonia in the right lung during the period in which I felt so sick.

The concern and determination of you people carried me through for I didn't even have the will to live at that point. Consider the fact that the pneumonia went away without being treated by so much as an aspirin tablet.

You must know how happy it makes me to write you now as a well man. Well enough and strong enough to accept responsibility for my own continuing state of health.

Ginnie and I now structure our days around three periods of meditation — morning, noon, and 5:00 PM. At these times we work on the last of the cancer and whatever other goals we have set for ourselves. Join us in spirit if you wish company in your meditations. We will know that you are there, as we sit by the fountain and the pebbles.

The job we set out to do nearly three months ago has been completed. Rejoice in your strength, and thank you for caring enough for a fellow traveler. Bless us all!

It may seem ironic now, after Aldie's death, to remember how sure he was then that he was a well man. Yet, at that time he really was. For three months he was "nine feet tall"— an Aldie-ism meaning confidence, achievement, and high energy flow. He was moving ahead rapidly on a glossary for marine botanists he wanted to publish, a project at the head of his wind-up-an-era list. He was enjoying the flurry of repair jobs on *Outward Bound,* our beloved sailing ketch on whom and with whom we lived for two months every summer in the Bahamas. He reveled in a sense of physical well-being, waking every morning to the thrill of just being alive. Most of all he was excited by the idea of responsibility for, and control over, his own disease; and by the power inherent in his own mind-body system. In the months that followed we were to come to a much deeper understanding of what that responsibility encompasses, not only in living but also in dying.

A dramatic remission seems to be a very common component of the cancer experience. It is a period that should perhaps be examined more closely. It is a time of brief reprieve for most patients, but for some the beginning of total freedom from the disease. No one knows why. Perhaps we need to question our simplistic assumptions about the nature of time in relation to the quality of life. Who would not give many years of gray half-life for three sparkling months of rebirth? Which is 'longer' in terms of eternity? Perhaps we miss the point when we distinguish between 'remission' and 'cure', although at the time I would have rejected such a suggestion out of hand. Probably the real question about such a period should be, "How is one's life changing? Is it leading in the direction of a victorious death no matter how many days or months or years away that is?"

Within two months Aldie had achieved a remarkable remission through the combined efforts of the radiation therapy and the energies of the Pebble People network. We believed the network's energy to be the more powerful tool. What we did not realize then was that healing does not always mean curing. Healing means more than the capacity to reverse the disease process.

Aldie believed that the remission period had been a gift from the Pebble People network and that without it he would not have been prepared for the next steps in his journey. The power of the Pebble People network enabled him to become strong enough to begin to accept responsibility for his own disease. He felt their work was complete.

It was time now for us to move forward, to understand more deeply the nature of personal responsibility and to create a new framework for our lives.

# Responsibility

CARL SIMONTON is a cancer specialist, trained in conventional therapies, who had the wit to do more than just notice that his patient's attitudes made a difference to their physiological responses to therapy. His determination to discover what kinds of mental images and beliefs made the difference and, more importantly, how a person can 'get' these beliefs, led him to develop a program that is cutting a swath through the cancer subculture. It is based on the idea that at some deeper-than-rational level of consciousness there is a pattern of responses, a mental and emotional orientation or a life-style, which creates the conditions for cancer as a response to certain life situations.

While the concept of responsibility for one's own illness shocks many people, it can come with the impact of a revelation, as it did for Aldie. If you have played some part in creating your own malignancy, clearly you have some measure of control over its progress. This concept alone can radically alter attitudes both toward the disease and the effects of conventional therapies. Carl feels that one can control one's physiological response to the radical therapies and is never surprised when patients in his program are free of damaging side effects. The program is a combination of group therapy, designed to uncover and change cancer-prone life patterns, and regular meditation of the 'mind control' type designed to energize the body's own immune system.

The group therapy involved three-day sessions four times a year. They were led by Carl and Stephanie, his wife and colleague, when we were in the program. These sessions outdid all the encounter groups and sensitivity training sessions I have ever participated in. Where most discourage husbands and wives from participating in the same group on the grounds that this makes it harder to free people from familiar patterns, Carl insists that his patients bring their spouses, or other significant persons. His reasoning is that the necessary changes will affect relationships with family members. For three full days six to ten people with death in their bodies, and their spouses, faced each other, hammering out sometimes very intimate responses. When habitual defenses went up, there was always someone to point out that we were playing for high stakes, for keeps, and there wasn't time for the usual games.

I have often thought since that the special genius of Carl and Stephanie lay in the fact that they were *not* professional encounter group leaders, *not* trained psychotherapists. They were successful because they cared. They really cared about every patient who worked with them and they let it show. They were also capable of using almost brutal questions in forcing self-analysis:

"Why did you want to die?"

"Why do you need to have cancer?"

"What deep need in your life is not being filled?"

"In what ways has life lost meaning for you?"

"Can you give two good reasons why you should be alive two years from now?"

They fought to give their patients confidence in the power of their own mind-body systems. They taught visualization techniques that required patients to picture their cancers in vivid detail (a very difficult task for those who were avoiding the reality), and to see the body's immune system mobilizing to conquer and destroy the cancer cells.

Working with Carl Simonton was, in a sense, a natural extension of the Pebble People network experience. Both were based on the assumption that there is energy in consciousness that can affect physiological processes. Carl's meditations tended to focus consciousness in very specific ways, adding the dimension of an individual's power over his own body. On the other hand, the Pebble People went a step beyond most scientists who are exploring mind-body linkages by assuming that there are linkages between people who love – transpersonal linkages through which a transfer of healing energy is possible.

Perhaps the image of 'training' for the events leading up to Aldie's death is too limited, too linear in the connotation of 'progress' toward a goal. In a way, the major experiences of those fifteen months were more like themes – themes in a symphony – introduced in one movement, dropped in favor of a second or third theme, and then recapitulated in one vast synthesis of themes at the end. The theme of the Pebble People network phase was synergy – the joining of many into one in such a way as to make each far greater than himself. The theme of the second phase was responsibility – the power of an individual to control and even create his own physiological reality. Two more themes were yet to come, surrender and acceptance; two more times we were to experience the painful conflict between these major themes, or major 'lessons'. They could even be considered as four different views of reality.

I have a great and abiding sympathy for those maligned 'cultists' who seek after THE truth, and having found one view of it, claim ultimacy and totality. I weep sometimes, in gentle envy, for the certainty, the clear-eyed singleness of purpose many of these people have. This coming to rest with a final formulation of reality had never been for us. We even flew a homemade burgee from the mainmast spreader on our sailboat that last summer with our private motto: *cavita vias,* "avoid pathways."

It had a vine on it to symbolize the jungle of belief systems that clamor for our allegiance and a machete to symbolize our determination to carve ourselves a new way.

We were not fully aware of the conflict between the theme of consensus and the theme of responsibility until the day, late that spring, that Aldie discovered a small inguinal node on his right leg. The next day, light from a window fell across his shoulder in such a way that I noticed a small swelling near the right clavicle. We stood together, our fingertips exploring the twin signals of metastasis, looking at each other with that sort of expressionlessness that masks internal gear-shifting. The nodes were small, like elongated marbles. We knew without even having to formulate the thoughts that although we had several months of active life still ahead, we had entered a new phase in our training.

In the first few days after we recognized the recurrence, I had to struggle against the sensation that somehow we had failed the Pebble People. I knew that there were many in the network who would feel that the recurrence of the cancer meant that our efforts had not 'worked'. I also knew that there were many who, having lost faith in traditional belief systems, yearned to believe that there is a source of energy that can be tapped for the healing of human bodies and human hearts. Some of these people seemed to me to be like tender new green shoots just lifting their heads into a new dimension and I could not bear the thought of their disillusionment. Aldie did not feel the way I did about having failed the Pebble People. We talked about writing them another letter to explain what had happened, but he could not find the right words. Only later, just before he died, was he able to put into words why the network had not failed.

We were asked by people in the network, and we continually asked ourselves during those first weeks after the recurrence, why we were not reactivating the network. The best either of us could do with it at the time was to simply say that it had been the appropriate response to the first onset of the disease, but that something else was needed for this second phase. Aldie intuitively turned toward an intensification of his efforts at personal responsibility for his own disease and the harnessing of his own mental energies to halt or reverse the disease process. Looking back now, I can see clearly how important it was for Aldie to have handled that second phase largely through his own efforts. This was where he learned at some very deep level that one does have control over one's own dying. It may seem odd to suggest that a person can learn how to control his dying by failing to control a disease.

The nodes continued to grow, slowly but inexorably, all through the summer cruise in the Bahamas. It could be asked why we let the whole summer go by without seeking any sort of physical therapy, radiation or chemotherapy. By this time Aldie not only *wanted* to believe that physiological processes are controlled by non-physical forces, as he had at the beginning, he *did* believe. He saw conventional physical therapies as just a way to buy time to make radical head and life-style changes that he thought would lead to a 'cancer free' life. The new nodes were not painful. He felt well enough to live our energetic life aboard *Outward Bound*, and he believed that intensified efforts to pour energy into his body's fight against the cancer was the way to go. Our second group session with Carl and Stephanie and other patients in Fort Worth was scheduled just before our departure on the boat. Carl supported Aldie's decision to delay physical therapy, though he would have supplied it if that is what Aldie had wanted. Our family physician Ken Swords also respected Aldie's decision, though perhaps more reluctantly.

The process of meditation had already begun to shift slightly for Aldie. At the beginning one decides rationally how one is to visualize the cancer, the action of the therapy, if any, and then the fighting behavior of the immune

system with its white blood cells. After a while the visualizations seem to take on a life of their own. Aldie would
often describe fascinating changes in the way the cancer
cells and white blood cells were interacting. I suppose
these could be called 'visions'. Just before we left on the
boat he told me about an event that cut through the visualizations and seemed to be of a different order of experience.

During one of his noontime meditations alone in his lab
at the Marine Institute, he said a voice 'broke through' his
visualizations speaking so rapidly as to go beyond the
boundary of language – even thought-language. It was as
if thoughts were being transmitted without the vehicle
of words. He felt a sensation of light and whorls as an
incredible amount of information was passed to him in a
split second.

When he told me about this experience, I thought of
Mozart, who could hear a whole symphony in one note and
then had to spend days and days laboriously writing it
down! Much of this information faded as time went by,
but one 'message' (if such it can be called) struck him
powerfully and permanently. Its import was that for Aldie
"mere interest is not enough – life for you requires enthusiasm." We had so often talked about his feeling of
having energy that was not being used up in his life, and
were both fascinated when we looked up the etymology
of the word "enthusiasm." It comes from the Greek *en-
theos,* meaning literally "in God," and is defined as "the
power actuating one who is inspired by a divine or super-
human power."

On the boat that summer he described a sensation of
"slipping back and forth between two dimensions." He
came down the companionway one day and said to me,
"Bujie, I think we are going to have to create a new reality."
Something rather awesome filled the cabin at that moment.
The idea that to some extent you can create your own reality
gives many people a sense of power and freedom, as it had
Aldie when we first began work with the Simontons. But

at that moment, we sensed that the new reality we were
to create would be costly.

Returning from the Bahamas late in August, we knew
that the two nodes were getting out of control. We flew
to Fort Worth, where Carl and Stephanie set aside two full
days for intensive sessions with just the four of us. During
these talks a crucial new direction in our transformation
began.

Early in the morning of the second day Aldie realized
with a shock that he was terrified of death. Using the
I'll-cope-with-it-when-the-time-comes approach, Aldie had
always been one of those people who don't want to think
seriously about death until they have to. In the months
since the cancer diagnosis, he had so focused on remission as an opportunity to make radical life changes that
he had not seen how much his motivation to live was
really his fear of death. The will to live, if it is to be a
healing force, must be unambiguous. Aldie realized that
his fear of death had lain unrecognized under his conscious
desire to live, undermining it. At the same moment he
realized something else which was importantly related
to his attitude toward death.

Not until that morning in Fort Worth did Aldie realize
that he had been using the same I-won't-think-about-it-
until-I-have-to approach toward the alternating pattern of
our relationship, forgetting the pain of the troughs as
soon as the joy of the next crest appeared. Aldie's ability
to forget the separateness so easily had been a source of
pain to me. Only much later, just as we were preparing for
the dying, was I to recognize the value of this 'failure'
on Aldie's part. It made Aldie cry that morning in the Fort
Worth motel, because he saw his response to pain as withdrawal, a self-imposed blindness that was somehow related
to his fear of death. He had always believed that when you
fear something, you are irresistably drawn toward it. So
he started to grapple with this fear in a characteristically
purposeful fashion.

Later that day, during the sessions with Carl and Stephanie, he explored his feelings and found that it was not so much death itself that he feared, but the 'humiliation and passivity' of a cancer death. As we talked about this, we decided to use a technique which had served us well through the years. We found that whenever we agreed upon something, if we verbalized it to the satisfaction of each and wrote it down, it invariably came to pass – though sometimes in rather surprising ways. It was our way of praying. Aldie wrote down what came out of discussing his fear of the passive death:

> We commit ourselves to an active participation in our own death process. We choose to die at home, not in a hospital. We intend to have full choice over the place and method of death (which might include illness) and we would want to cooperate with Him in selecting the time. Ginnie chooses to die while awake, I want to die in my sleep. Ginnie looks forward to death as a positive experience. I would like to feel positive about the death experience as a transition from one good to a different good. I do not now feel this way but I feel acceptance of the reality of death is a necessary experience for us all. I feel, too, that I will become more 'porous' to these thoughts as the block [the fear of death] recedes.

As I began to face my terror at the idea of separation, we discovered that this was also part of Aldie's fear – a dying person is as afraid of separation from loved ones as those who must face life alone. While talking about separation and the way that we loved each other, a very curious thing happened in that little conference room. Aldie and I turned to face each other, and suddenly it felt as if we were in some other space or dimension. I remember being aware of Carl and Stephanie across the table, but somehow, they had receded. We were saying things we didn't even know we knew, and afterwards we couldn't remember exactly what we had said to each other. All we could reconstruct was that we agreed we had to strengthen that part of our unity which could not die. Building on each other's half-thoughts and halting phrases, we spoke of having to get to that place inside ourselves where we were one — where we could never be separated, where life and death were one, and "where it wouldn't matter whether we lived or died." Speaking that phrase simultaneously, we both experienced a sense of great discovery and joy. At the same time, though, there was an awesome feeling, as if we had verbalized a goal that was way beyond ourselves. For some curious reason, the four of us left that room feeling as if a good decision had been made, a difficult problem resolved.

Looking back, I see that moment as the turning point — the point at which we stepped beyond the limitations of the psychological approach, beyond the concept of individual responsibility, and even beyond the hope that Aldie would live. The search for a new reality that would tap Aldie's unused energy which had sustained us, was transmuted into something else — the realization that the major life change we faced was death. It took many months of struggle for us to grasp this, to really believe and accept what we had said.

While it may seem that Aldie's death negates the efficacy and transforming power of Carl's program, the truth is quite the opposite. We met several cancer patients who, through Carl's program, had been turned away from death and set on the path to a permanent remission. But for those, like Aldie, whose path would lead to death, Carl offered a re-orientation in consciousness that altered the experience of dying. Aldie counted Carl his best medical advisor and a true friend all through the last year of his life. He sought the counsel and comfort that Carl could give right up until the time he could no longer talk on the phone. While Aldie was dying, I tried to tell Carl and Stephanie that his death should not be interpreted as a failure. But, oriented as they are to saving, or at least prolonging, active life, it must be hard for them to see a fulfilling death as anything but second best.

I shall always be grateful for the part Carl and Stephanie played in our struggle. Just as the Pebble People network had helped us begin our journey by reinforcing our belief in the power of love—the belief that lay at the core of our life together; Carl and Stephanie brought us through the second stage, turning us inward to accept personal responsibility and create our own reality. The greatest benefit of the Simonton program was not so much in the control of the disease or in psychological explorations, helpful though these were. The most important contribution to our lives was the initiation of regular meditation times each day. Though we began meditating with the Pebble People network, Carl's program expanded it to a three-times-a-day routine which took precedence over any other schedule. This was the closest we ever came to a satisfying structure for the spiritual aspect of our love.

Many experienced meditators, especially of the Eastern disciplines, consider mind-control, goal-oriented visualization to be an inferior approach to the spiritual life. To us it seemed that it didn't matter much how one began. The regularity of the meditation seemed to set in motion a process which gradually affected the quality of our consciousness. Deeper levels of meditation experiences began to appear spontaneously. Within the Christian framework of beliefs, the same process could be said to occur with regular times of prayer. Prayer or meditation, use what method you will, the journey into inner space begins, and it is there that one finds the strength and understanding to accept death's transformation.

# Surrender

AFTER THOSE FOUR revealing days in Fort Worth, we planned to leave for Minnesota where a family reunion had been planned. Our discovery in Fort Worth—that it didn't matter whether we lived or died, that the end of our search was death—seemed to fade from consciousness as we moved away from the clinic. There are truths too brilliant to be looked at for long. The intuition that we would have to surrender to what death would do to our love was more than we could handle—except in flashes—during the next six months. In between we were like creatures caught in a trap, twisting and turning to find some means of escape. The twists and turns may seem futile in retrospect, but each forced us to grow a little, making us stronger and more able to face the Clear Light.

There was a great deal of conflict in our minds between the responsibility-control theme and the newer theme of surrender—of reaching for that place in our love which is beyond life or death. As this conflict increased, so did the pain in Aldie's shoulder. We thought then that it was caused by the pressure of the node near the right clavicle on a nerve network. Aldie had begun to take medication for the pain, a codein-based pill, but was not ready to subject himself to further radiation or chemotherapy. He had investigated a suggestion of Carl's involving immunology, but that had turned out to be disappointing. By the time of our family reunion on the beautiful shores of Lake Superior, the internal battle between responsibility and surrender was raging. Aldie still searched himself for causes and still talked in terms of life-style changes that could lead to a cancer-free life. The family asked for a full-scale meeting at the reunion so everyone could hear "straight from the horse's mouth" exactly where Aldie stood, physically and mentally.

We gathered one morning, all eleven of us; our five children, Tip, Ric, Julie, Connie, and Jennifer; two in-laws, Ric's beautiful wife Molli, and Joey who is married to Julie; and two grandchildren, Charlie and Sean, Ric and Molli's sons. We sat in creaking wicker chairs on the front porch of an antique northwoods cabin. Lake Superior lapped gently at the rocks just outside the screens and the musty smell of mildewed grass rugs perfumed the air. Aldie explained exactly what the two new nodes were doing, where the pain was coming from, how the immunology hopes had fizzled out, and what could be expected from more radiation and chemotherapy.

No one in the family had much faith in physical therapies. They were dismissed as merely ways to buy more time. I think that Molli knew then that Aldie had had his last new lease on life. She pleaded only for him to "make his peace with God," apologizing for her 'old-fashioned' phrase, but unable to find one that suited her purpose better. The others pressed Aldie to "take the initiative" — "Tell us what you want us to do or think." There was enormous pressure on Aldie to continue in the subtle, persuasive, but firm leadership role he had always held in the family. Aldie was forced to say in a variety of ways that he simply didn't know where to lead us. Sitting in our wicker chairs, we were throwing ourselves against the limits of our control over what was happening to us.

The suggestion was made that Aldie and I live apart for a week or two in order to find our separate selves. We rejected that idea out of hand. At one point, Joe told Aldie, "I will accept your decision to die if that is what you want to do, but I won't let you go unless you can tell me why."

Aldie was very upset at the implication that he was choosing to die. And yet, it was he who had been so excited about
the idea that he had participated in the creation of his
own disease.

Tip finally pushed the responsibility theme to its ultimate, coming dangerously close to a truth all of us had
skirted. He spotted Aldie on a rather graceful pretense
he had used for a couple of years—that he was really working full time at his profession. This was a bit of pretense
in which the family had silently concurred, protecting
ourselves, and Aldie, from the knowledge that his second
career was not a satisfying one. He had left a successful
business life to go back to college for retraining in his
first love—marine botany. Seven years as a middle-aged
student, however, capped by an academic hassle over the
granting of his PhD, had left their scars. He never really
gave the energy of which he was capable to his new work.
It was a taut moment when Tip put his finger on this painful truth, but Aldie managed to steer the conversation
subtly back to more comfortable paths.

Something had shifted in the relationship between Aldie and Tip during that brief moment, however. Aldie
experienced Tip's love for him in a new way after that
confrontation. Tip was seventeen when Aldie and I were
married; and Aldie had always assumed the three older
children loved him because he was the man their mother
loved. After that meeting, Aldie told me with a sense of
real wonder that he'd never realized until then that Tip
loved him for himself and not just because of me. Tip's
courage in laying bare Aldie's vulnerable spot had proved
his love, even though Aldie was not able to pursue the
thought.

That family meeting could be marked as the beginning
of a process that was important to Aldie's fulfillment in
death. Gradually, over the last four months of his life,
each of his significant relationships was brought to some
sort of resolution or fulfillment—a moment of courageous

honesty, a restraint removed, a pretense laid aside, un-spoken love spelled out. Perhaps the process of surrender is set in motion even before the conscious act is possible.

We left that morning meeting to pursue our separate pleasures as our various interests took us—to tennis court, beach, deertrack, and rental sailboat. It is wonderful how naturally tragedy and pleasure can blend. Death came to that family reunion, but it did not spoil our fun or our unself-conscious enjoyment of each other.

Aldie was still looking back into his life for answers to the deeper 'whys'. Perhaps it was Tip's hard truth that set him thinking about enthusiasm, that state of being *en-theos*, which he had lost and tried so unsuccessfully to regenerate over the years. Two days later he made this journal entry:

> I believe this morning that the major contributing factor to my illness is my continuing loss of enthusiasm, for with enthusiasm has always come an abiding and sustaining sense of determination and confidence. In fact, in my opinion, this enthusiasm has been my 'hallmark' all my life.
>
> Somewhere the ability to enthuse must have been lost and I think this has to do with the difficulty over the PhD. During, or just at the end of, this period my confidence was broken and this carried away the enthusiasm and determination with it.
>
> For the last five years since then the only real bout of enthusiasm I can readily recall had to do with buying and commissioning *Outward Bound*—although I suspect the thrill lasted through the second and maybe the third summers with reduced intensity. I still love the boat—it is part of my life—but this is not quite the same thing.
>
> Enthusiasm and confidence are a strong combination, for with them the petty arguments and disagreements and misunderstandings are either impossible or irrelevant. Without enthusiasm, at least in sustaining amounts, so many things can erode the ego and damage what confidence is left.
>
> I think these things particularly in relation to Ginnie, for to the degree that I have lost my ability to 'get it on' I have lost the very thing that attracted her in the first place, and the thing that she had looked forward to benefiting

from over the years – spiritual leadership.

Solving the mechanics of interpersonal relationships is a highly desirable and necessary goal for it makes life more enjoyable and frees two people to live more aspects of life together – it allows them to be closer and warmer. It does not, however, offer a new lease on life and I do not believe it will save mine. I do not believe it is too late for saving enthusiasm but I do not know in what area to look for it.

It is one thing to accept the reality of death, and I think I have moved a bit along this path after a slow start. It is quite another thing to grasp the significance of death as a possibility within a comparatively short time – a few months. The human mind, at least mine, almost refuses this information.

I think now that the self analysis and the search for psychological whys was valuable as a sort of life-review process. I think also that it was important for Aldie to pinpoint the time his dying began – not because it could change anything, but because a life needs to be seen for what it was before it can be laid reverently aside.

It was the family football game the next day, which Aldie watched from the sidelines holding his aching arm and shoulder, that brought him to the realization that he really was going to die. Perhaps it was the symbolism of the chance setting. We were ten assorted bodies hurtling ourselves at each other on the slippery turf, calling outrageous plays, and gulping with laughter as the final plays degenerated into freeze tag. At one end of the field were some rickety bleachers where Aldie sat watching us through a high link fence, dividing the kaleidoscopic movement on one side from the huddled immobility on the other.

That night was Julie's "golden" birthday party – she was twenty-nine on the twenty-ninth of August. Aldie and I were standing by the sink making a special salad. For a brief moment we were alone in the kitchen, and he said, "I realized this afternoon that I am going to die."

Such a simple sentence! Such little words!

That evening was something out of some other world. It was like a slow-motion charade. We had all gotten as dressed up as you can get on a vacation where eleven people are strewn about the floors of a northwoods summer cabin in sleeping bags, sharing one bathroom. We had all gotten gifts together for Julie and wrapped them in everything from birchbark to aluminum foil. Molli, our culinary genius, had somehow produced a chocolate layer cake and the table was laden with special goodies. But, by the time dinner was ready, the charade had begun. Aldie's recognition of his impending death had begun to penetrate the family circle. First one, and then another heard what he had said. When Molli heard, she went to put her arms around him and they stood hugging for a brief moment in the kitchen. She told me later, that for the first time, she felt as if he had let her all the way into the very inside of him.

Shaken by his realization, Aldie drank too much scotch and kept reaching for cigarettes – which he had dearly loved all his life, but had given up with the lung cancer diagnosis. This brought out responses of fear and distress in varying degrees in different members of the family. We took turns sitting with Aldie out on the dock in the darkness where he alternately spoke out his fears and wept his grief.

Inside the house there was genuine celebration of Julie's birthday. Amid laughter over the gifts and people carrying laden plates to some convenient perch, temporary clusters of two or three would form to hold each other briefly, murmuring words of comfort or wiping away tears. Everyone, including our eleven- and twelve-year-old grandsons, circulated both spatially and emotionally during the evening – now gobbling food with appreciation on the miniscule dining porch, now laughing over gifts by the fire in the living room, now standing briefly in the shadows holding someone for comfort, or sitting with Aldie on the dock sharing the pain of his fear and grief. We watched the alcohol dissolve his grief into self-pity, knowing this, too, was part of his way. I remember thinking, as I moved through the little log cabin house, how it was like a stage set with many different scenes being played out simultaneously under separate spotlights – the players moving from lighted circle through the shadows to lighted circle.

For some of the family that night marked their knowing that Aldie would die within three or four months. For others, including Aldie and me, the realization sank again under the determination of hope. Recognition of death's imminence did not come upon us gradually. It came like a series of thunderous tidal waves that engulfed us and then receded, leaving us struggling back to the shore, certain that we could cling to the familiar sands.

Looking back, it seems unbelievable that we continued to cast about for some radical change in our life-style that would reverse the course of the disease. Aldie had already said in so many words that he knew he was going to die. We both had verbalized our knowledge that the transformation we had sensed, even before the cancer, was going to take us far beyond the physical and psychological realms, that the changes must be essentially spiritual. We had even committed ourselves to finding that state of union beyond what we had known – where it wouldn't matter whether we lived or died.

Yet we kept searching for some easier transformation than death. We had still not given up the hope that we could find a way to change our lives so that Aldie would not have to die. Surrender came hard for us both. We fought it in three ways during the next three months. One was almost heroic, one very conventional, and one utterly ridiculous.

The first was an attempt to subject ourselves to an entirely different belief system in the radically altered life-style of an Indian ashram.

While we were in Minnesota, friends had introduced us to a psychoanalyst noted for his use of meditation and other approaches to higher states of consciousness. The psychoanalyst told us about Swami Rama, an East Indian guru of impressive reputation. He had cooperated with Dr. Elmer Green of the Menninger Clinic in the widely publicized scientific documentation of a yogi's remarkable control over supposedly involuntary physiological processes – heartbeats, blood pressure, body temperature, brain waves, glandular activity, etc. The psychoanalyst suggested that since we were "dabbling around the edges of higher states of consciousness and spiritual power," we might as well go straight to the heart of the matter and contact Swami Rama. I was excited, seeing the possibilities in spiritual disciplines that lead to control of physical states. Aldie, on the other hand, hesitated, sensing in the Eastern way a new dimension that might lead in an entirely different direction. As he tried to analyze his feelings about fear of death and his resistance to meeting with Swami Rama, Aldie made this entry in our common journal:

After talking with Swami Rama, I feel as if I am being accepted into a larger world – a more universal, an older world than I have experienced before, and I am kicking and protesting all the way. Because it is unfamiliar in its dimensions, it is frightening.

I now feel as if my life has reached a crossroads, but there is no choice of paths for me to make – the choice has been made elsewhere. I don't know which road I am to take, to death or to life, and never have I felt more unprepared to walk either. The lore I have built up, my knowledge, my experience – being limited to a smaller world view – may not sustain me in these new dimensions.

On the other hand the fear of asking Swami whether this disease carries me forward to transition or to a 'reborn' life has lost its malevolence in my mind. Nothing he could say would change a destiny already ordained. Foreknowledge of my future would make the experience, whichever it is to be, the richer and more rewarding.

Until now I have been convinced that I could handle a crisis with quiet strength. This has been sustaining – a matter of ego-strength. I have liked this quality in me.

Part of this fear generated now is the equally deep-seated conviction that I am faced with a world in which this is not enough; what worked before won't work now. 'Fighting' with humility – giving myself over to someone else's strength – has never been my bag. Now, however, surrender makes more sense, and even has a warm feeling to it. I must be changing.

There is a conflict in me for I cannot yet reconcile these various views with those of Carl Simonton with whom I identify. He, in my understanding at least, would have me fight to the end for life – for a goal of my choosing.

I am still afraid of death and I am still afraid of pain – the former because it seems so remote and strange, the latter because it is so close.

The conflict between the themes of responsibility and surrender drove a wedge between us. I believe now that a recurrent problem for any family facing death, oddly enough, is the issue of hope. Hope is the bright bird we must always keep in sight, shining through the darkness of the jungle. To follow it we must learn that its plumage changes. What we hope *for* must evolve. Until now, our hope had been based on the idea that we could *do* something to make Aldie live. Hope and life were synonymous.

Our whole focus had been on living, on attempting to reverse the disease process – first with the Pebble People through the power of love, and later with the Simontons through the power of personal responsibility. Yet the concept of responsibility in self-healing can be a double-edged sword. When in spite of all your efforts, the cancer continues to grow, it is often experienced as failure. There can be feelings of self-blame, inadequacy, and powerlessness. I felt that we had failed the Pebble People. My response to this sense of failure was to renew our efforts in any way that was suggested. I was desperately hoping for change.

Aldie's hesitation in contacting Swami Rama seemed like a foot-dragging and it made me angry. I think now that it was at this point that Aldie's goals began to shift, though he had no words for it. Together, in Fort Worth, we had glimpsed a hope that lay beyond the hope for life and health. But I was still clinging to the more limited goal. Somewhere deep inside, Aldie was beginning to surrender to something beyond life. It was more than just the passive 'acceptance of death' that we are all supposed to come to sooner or later. He tried to say it one night while we were floundering about in our separateness over calling Swami Rama. He'd been thinking about surrender and what it meant, and said in an almost awed tone, "You know, I've just realized that I'm going to have to make the same sorts of changes whether I live or die. Living well and dying well are the same thing! They require identical changes!" As he said that, I remembered our "it wouldn't matter" dialogue in Fort Worth just two weeks before and felt as if I were standing on the edge of a deep chasm filled with mists. I think we both sensed that we were moving into a new place where neither of us had ever been.

Aldie finally decided to call Swami Rama and made arrangements for us to stay in his Himalayan Institute just outside of Chicago for ten days. We told each other we were subjecting ourselves to this experience in order to learn new tools, spiritual disciplines that could transform us. I see now that we were both ambivalent about just what kind of transformation we expected. Also, though neither of us would have admitted it, I think that deep down we each harbored a childish hope that Swami Rama could do magic, and would bail us out with a physical miracle!

We were supposed to have stayed ten days, but the experience reduced us to such shambles that we left at the end of a week. We had come expecting some in-depth interaction with Swami Rama. What we got was a glimpse of the great man as he touched down briefly at the Chicago Institute between trips to his other institutes in Paris and Japan!

He spent all of ten minutes with Aldie and ten seconds

nodding to me in the hall. Who knows whether this was lack of concern or an intuitive awareness of our real needs? Even as we were busy being angry at him, we realized that, in the hands of the subordinate staff, we were getting exactly what we had asked for—a radical change in both conceptual system and life style. At the same time, we resisted like two recalcitrant children.

Our days were structured for us from 5:45 AM until 11 PM with hatha yoga, breathing and relaxation exercises, meditation, biofeedback training for brainwave control, countless lectures by Swami (on tapes!), endless glasses of carrot juice, un-gourmet vegetarian cookery, and just one cup of tea per day.

The pain in Aldie's right arm and shoulder was becoming intense, frighteningly so. The fact that he *knew* his resistance to the ashram experience was intensifying the pain didn't help one bit! He could not participate at all in the yoga and had to do everything else flat on his back. We were bitterly amused that the only comfortable position he could find is known in yoga circles as the 'corpse posture'. Aldie's rebellion was expressed largely in hating the food. He would nearly weep with yearning over the thought of a cup of coffee. The only thing we both responded to with enthusiasm was the biofeedback machines. We found they deepened and enriched our meditation experience which had become very important to us.

I loved the hatha yoga and am still grateful for that week's training. Curiously (or is it?), the thing I resisted the most was being told precisely what I myself had defined as my own goal—to find that place in myself where Aldie and I were one, beyond our bodies and beyond our emotions and beyond our minds. At the institute we were bombarded by a belief system that offered freedom from suffering through transcendence and detachment. "Detachment" is a hard, hard word for two people who had sought and found salvation through a human attachment that amounted to mutual identification. At one point, frightened by Aldie's increasing disability, I came all apart at the seams, completely submerged in panic at the total separation I sensed ahead. The noises I was making sounded more animal than human as I tried to keep them confined to our little room. The doctor on the institute staff found me in this condition and, with true inner serenity, told me to use the breathing exercises I had been taught and to learn to experience myself as the Self behind my physical, mental, emotional, and psychological self – the Self in which Aldie and I were one with the All. He was almost using the same words Aldie and I had used during that transforming dialogue in Fort Worth in August. But at that moment, I hated him for his serenity. I could not bear the thought of unity with Aldie through merging with the All. I didn't give a damn about the All. Aldie was my All and I was going to lose him, and the world was pain, pain, pain. I have since been to that place the wise doctor tried to show me, but the twin keys of surrender and humility are not always near at hand. I still resist detachment as the Way, for I know love as total attachment and I cannot reconcile the two. I suspect that the mutual surrender of two people to each other in love leads ultimately to the same All which Eastern mystics seek through detachment, but the paths seem irreconcilable. Trying to subject myself to the Hindu belief system was no mere experiment. It was the crashing, wrenching collision of two experiental opposites – a gut-trip, not a head-trip. But I made a decision that week. If I have to choose between detached serenity and pain I will still choose pain, for that is where most of my fellow human beings seem to be – and shared pain leads to love.

The collision which was throwing us into such turmoil was not just a matter of exploding beliefs. It also had to do with the structure of interpersonal relationships. We were immersed in a hierarchically structured world, the antithesis of everything we strived for in our family and professional lives. While we could appreciate the genius of the structure for the transmission of spiritual disciplines, we suffered horribly from a sense of being one-down—a blow to our already shaken self-esteem. In fact, it was impossible for us to avoid the feeling that we had committed an egregious spiritual boo-boo by having tangled with cancer in the first place. There was the insidious feeling that anyone who gets sick is somehow a spiritual failure. I could not help but contrast this with the compassion and loving support which flowed through the Pebble People network.

This pervasive sense of failure was probably inspired more by Aldie's deteriorating condition than by anything said by the people at the institute. Perhaps it was also an inevitable side effect of the inner conflicts as we struggled to find meaning in disease and death.

Leaving Chicago, we flew straight to Fort Worth. Aldie's pain was debilitating, the tumors growing so fast we were measuring them with a paper template! After tests, Carl Simonton started Aldie on three weeks of radiation, a second attempt to stave off surrender which was as useless as it was conventional. Aldie knew it would only buy a little time. We didn't realize how little. However short, though, it did give us a comfortable kind of respite.

We settled ourselves into the kitchenette-motel room with which we had become quite familiar on previous visits. Again, the radiation worked quickly, reducing the pain considerably after the first week, and again there were no side effects at all. What Aldie had needed from the Pebble People during the first period of radiation nearly a year before, he was able this time to do for himself. He spoke often of the complete confidence he had in his own ability to control his body's response to the radiation and of the gratitude he felt for the Pebble People who had proved to him that it was possible.

Our world became very small—a motel room filled with beautiful weeds from untended lots nearby. I conducted daily sorties in search of new weeds and the beer bottles to put them in. The natives of this particular section of Fort Worth apparently drink beer by the quart, twisting the bottles into ubiquitous brown paper bags and then tossing them into vacant lots as they cruise in their cars. Our days centered around the daily trip to the radiation center, by taxi for the first ten days and then on foot as Aldie began to feel stronger. We became connoisseurs of the local educational TV station, and I developed impressive calf muscles striding home with bags of groceries from the store a mile away. We talked of changes we were going to make, based on our ashram experience, still hoping for a transformation short of death.

As I write, I think fondly of those three weeks in the motel-room cocoon, where our minds and hearts seemed to be weaving themselves into an ever-tighter, two-person mesh. We saw a TV special one night based on the life of Babe Didrikson, who died of cancer, and Aldie burst into tears watching the deathbed scene between the Babe and her husband. It was pretty Hollywood, but it hit close to home. Some of the agony of separation swept over Aldie, and he talked again of how he didn't fear death itself, but the humiliation of body and especially the separation. I cannot help but wonder if the dead feel the separation as searingly as the dying – or the survivors. I hope not. I hope that death brings the broader vision that keeps one more permanently in the unity beyond separation.

It is a wonder to me that in October we could still be talking so confidently about creating a cancer-free life-style and at the same time weep together with the dreadful foretaste of separation. I guess this is the strange pheno-menon of hope – the hope that sustains, and often is so hard to distinguish from denial. Hope is a special sort of blindness. But, if you are open to it, the blindness can give you second sight – lead you to experience another reality beyond our little three-dimensional world of logic. In that other reality hope is altered and death is not the terrifying end it seems.

For Aldie that other reality was beginning to open up during that last time in Fort Worth. He had several meditations that could be called visions or hallucinations – experiences which were of the death time and probably preparation for it. Both of us had had deeper meditations since the ashram and the biofeedback training, and had sensed 'presences' when we got to that place which is deep meditation. The 'presences' were plural and were not exactly shapes. Aldie said they shouldn't be described visually – "just as shadows and warmth." But on two occasions he described such detailed experiences that I wrote them down. One occurred under the huge Van de Graff X-ray generator. Always spending fifteen or twenty minutes in what he called 'pre-meditation' before the treatment, Aldie then went into his deeper meditation state under the machine. On this particular day he dictated this description immediately afterward:

> I don't know why the meditation changed, and there was certainly no warning. When I began, I felt as usual that I was dropping down to the deeper levels. Today, however, I was a participant rather than an observer in my own treatment. As a disembodied, weightless presence, I was commingled with the tumor and the X rays in slowly undulating, warm clouds of gold, yellow, orange, and brown tones. There were frequent sparkles. I had the sensation of being rolled over and over but it did not bring fear or anxiety. Perhaps most important, there was no sensation of pain whatsoever in my normally aching shoulder and arm.
>
> As each four minute period progressed, the undulating clouds, accompanied by tones rather than distinct music, grew smaller, and at the end it appeared as if the tumors had been consumed. When the singing of the generator ceased, indicating the end of treatment, a viscous wall or river of white blood cells flowed swiftly across this otherwise undefined area, closing like the seas coming together. As they receded again, all evidence of debris from the tumors had been removed by them and trails of white blood cells spiraled slowly off into the dark, presumably following blood vessels to the liver and kidneys.

As the mop-up was completed, the coloration of the area turned to shades of blue and I noted that there were small patches or blobs of white blood cells still remaining. One by one, these assumed a star shape and exploded, shooting rivers of white cells out through the entire body, policing the entire system. This seemed to happen in pulsing waves.

There was something paradoxical. At the edge of the undefined space I was in, there were walls of white blood cells waiting, walls and rivers, yet the space was not defined. There was no consciousness of the room I was in. There was no machine, no table. The singing sound of the machines became part of the music in my cosmos. It was spacelessness and yet there was space.

A week later a similar sort of vision or fantasy occurred while he was 'pre-meditating' alone in the coffee room:

This happened sometime in the future, I don't know when. I could see myself lying in bed, in Miami. I was very sick with cancer and the pain was very strong. The time was perhaps two o'clock in the morning. I remember awakening sharply from a fitful doze. I called to Ginnie, rather loudly I thought. I asked her to make ready a tape recorder for, as I told her, "the moment of choice had come." She miraculously arranged a rather large one within a matter of minutes. As the struggle between life and death began, I kept trying to talk to her and, at times, to answer questions she asked.

I felt at this time in a wholly disembodied state floating above myself. I did not again return to my body until the struggle was over, but I was not aware that I went very far away.

I could tell, and I think Ginnie could tell, which side of the choice I was on because as I undulated upside-down for the death state and right side-up for the living state, the language I had available to me changed. It was normal English in the living state, but I don't know what language it was for the other.

It was very apparent to me that the cards were stacked against living. When I rolled into the living position (face up), the pain returned two-fold. In the death position there was no pain at all.

One interesting thing was that death presented me with a re-experience of things in childhood. The life side apparently offered equal inducements but they must have been in a different realm. I didn't even know what they were then. They seemed attractive but I couldn't see what they were.

I don't know as the basis for the choice was ever clearly stated but I chose for life, ending a two-hour struggle. I returned to my body and the pain returned to me.

Some of the images Aldie described were so like what we saw and heard as he lay dying two and one-half months later, that I still ponder these visions' function and the meaning of his 'choice for life'.

A few weeks after this experience, when the weakness and pain returned, he said a most interesting thing to me. His eyes were very large and clear and his voice was very strong as he said, "Don't worry about these physical effects —that is not what is the matter. We must never, never again mistake the physical effects for the real disease. The real struggle is in the mind, and behind the mind where I cannot even see it or understand it. It is like dark clouds rolling. The struggle is between darkness and light." I marveled that such words were coming from the man who, fifteen months before, had only *wanted* to believe in the power of consciousness to affect the body.

After we came home from Fort Worth, there were two marvelous weeks when Aldie felt a little of his old interest in life, and we charged off into yet another escape from the real task before us. We tried the cancer diet—seven pints of vegetable juices a day, nothing else. Even as we chased each other in and out of the bathroom, we had to laugh at what was happening to us. We learned beyond a shadow of a doubt that if head changes affect the body, the reverse is also true! Radical dietary changes can really mess up your head. We snapped at each other for no reason, and I wept copious and unexplainable tears into the endless sacks of carrots I juiced. It took only two weeks of this for us to modify the diet, albeit with new respect for the bumper stickers proclaiming, "you are what you eat"!

I have to say that, ineffective as it was for Aldie, this absurd experiment was an invaluable experience for me. It was so traumatic and so drastic a break in lifelong eating habits – I swear it re-programmed my taste buds – that it left me free to re-structure my relationship with my own body.

We were just recovering from the diet when Thanksgiving came. At Thanksgiving the end really began, and we stopped trying to fight the cancer. "There comes a time," Aldie said, "when you have to quit fighting and roll with the disease." The time had come for surrender. Having explored all sorts of transforming power sources outside of ourselves, we finally came back to where we had started – with the Pebble People and the power of love within. But before I could return to this wellspring I had some debris to clear away. I had to come to terms with the reality of anger.

# From Anger
# to Acceptance

WE WENT TO BE WITH Joe and Julie for the Thanksgiving holiday in the foothills of the Blue Ridge Mountains where they live. Jennifer came from boarding school and Tim came from college. Tim, Aldie's son and my stepson, had been a beloved sailing companion for parts of five summers. In fact, the six of us who gathered for that holiday shared the unspoken secrets of people who had lived at sea together – people who have sweated together, yawned on night watches together, worshipped sunsets together, heard the rigging sing together, and gone cold with sudden fear together. Only such people could have watched Aldie and me as the pain set in again Thanksgiving night. Only they could have had the courage to tell us that the time had come for us to go apart for awhile. The whole family had suggested this at the reunion, but we could not hear them then. For nearly twenty years we had loved best the times when we could be together twenty-four hours a day, seven days a week. We couldn't have imagined a reason to be apart during the most severe test of our loving. At Thanksgiving I still found it hard to believe that they were right, but Aldie knew and he insisted on going home three days before I did. Joe and Julie allowed me to follow only after I had promised to go down to the Florida Keys for another week alone. I finally agreed, thinking that I would take materials for a seminar I was to teach in January and use the time to do some necessary planning. I still could not face squarely the real purpose of our time apart.

This time apart came in two sections – my three days in Virginia with Joe and Julie after Jennifer, Tim, and Aldie left, and the week in the Keys. Though I could not name them until they were completed, I had two tasks, each requiring a different environment. Before I could even approach my final surrender, I had to face the final purge of my anger. As it turned out, Joey had to accomplish this first task as well.

Joey was working on a play based on the August reunion experiences, and we planned to use my extra three days in Virginia to discuss some problems he was having. Every morning after Julie left for work, Joey and I would settle down to his manuscript, but in a matter of minutes it would be forgotten as we heatedly discussed the patterns of Aldie's life that had made him susceptible to cancer and what we wished he were doing about them! For three days we talked nonstop, only at the end realizing the incredible depths of the anger we'd spilled onto each other. Oh, when scholars analyze the processes of dying and bereavement and speak of anger, they speak the truth! Anger is the most corrosive and painful part of the total agony, and it must be faced. It must.

In some people it may come out as anger at God, anger at the doctors, anger at other family members for imagined neglect, or even anger at the dying person. For the dying person it can be anger at the survivors. The object of the anger differs with every person facing a death – his own or a beloved's. Joey and I discovered that we were angry at Aldie, terribly, powerfully angry. I suspect we were not unique in our rage at the dying for leaving us. Who knows if this is entirely irrational? If we do have some deep-level choice in the time and manner of our own deaths, then to some extent we are truly choosing to leave this life and our loved ones. Those we leave behind must deal with their anger before they can glimpse some larger purpose, some greater love in our leaving.

I now realize that by Thanksgiving everyone else in the family, including Julie, understood that Aldie was going to die soon. But Joey and I were still hanging on, holding out, certain that the tide could be held back, certain that if Aldie would only grasp the power of his potential and fling himself into its fulfillment, he would be saved.

Aldie's undisciplined creativity was as apparent to him as it was to us. He had left so many discoveries about his favorite species of marine plants undocumented. But more important to us were the might-have-beens we couldn't even name. Aldie knew how to break the bonds of conventional thought, to escape the confines of his culture, but he never stepped across the threshhold into the act of creation that should have followed. There was about him such a sense of unfulfilled potential. For this we were angry at him – Joey and I – angry to the depths of our need for him. Joey sent me his journal, written just after Aldie died, in which he recorded the anger uncovered in those three days.

> Aldie was the stuff from which myth is created. His was a great mind which was never used. He was a man of many dreams who settled on none of them. He was a creature of whim as well as whimsy, of indulgence as well as the most formidable of asceticisms, of logic as well as legerdemain which baffled all of us on many an occasion. Yet he was a man in essential harmony with the world and himself, secure in an equilibrium between stimulus and response – a man at home and at peace with an existence he did not create. Yet he lost that security, was thrown out of equilibrium, and finally actively sought to end what was no longer a tenable existence.
>
> After a week of intensive anger, anger which was released by Mom, I was, for awhile, willing to sacrifice my entire relationship with Aldie in one last ditch stand against the inevitable. That was how I viewed it. His death was vicious and unnecessary pain to be suffered by us because he dared to turn away from this earth which we inhabit. I had always told him that I would fight him bitterly and without rules to the very end. I told him I would sacrifice anything to keep him alive, that I was greedy, that I was

selfish, that I was not easily thwarted. I believe it was that which later kept him asking if I would be angry at his dying – which kept him wondering if I would refuse to shed the burden of my own pride. Because I loved him as a man. I loved him. I loved him. There will never be another Aldie. I can never love another man as I loved him. There is no opening of that door a second time. But that is as it should be. For I must cherish what I have had. Aldie once said that I was the angriest man he had ever known – and my anger was greater as his death approached than it had ever been before. I was swathed in it and devoured by it. I had only to think of what was coming to feel its irrational upwellings. I told him so many times that I would always regret our not having been of the same age. I told him this even before the cancer came. I told him this when I thought of all those days he had lived without me, and even of those I had lived without him. And then the cancer came to take the man I loved above all others while he was not yet old and I was still young.

Aldie would have been cruelly hurt had he heard Joey and me rail at him those three days – exposing all his failures, all his impotence with our words. And yet, we had to do it. We had to metabolize that anger, digest its bitterness, and so let it permeate our beings. Only in that way could it be transmuted into the powerful love inherent in such anger. Oddly, as I write this, I realize that Joey and I were going through the same process that Aldie and I had discovered as the way to love our children – a way to stop the subtle chain of destruction in which the sins of the fathers are unwittingly, unconsciously visited upon the sons unto endless generations. We purged ourselves of our angers, whatever the source and however justified, by raging together and sometimes at each other. Together we became sort of a sponge which soaked up the accumulation of angers that are so easily displaced onto others. What then spilled out onto the children was only love and the natural limitations set by realistic needs, rather than the force of anger masquerading as parental discipline – or lack of it. In the same manner Joey and I were saving

Aldie from the full force of our anger at him – anger that will always express itself in subtle ways no matter how successfully denied. If death, as so many say, is intertwined with love, then it is equally intertwined with anger. With death comes a sense of outrage which must be squarely faced and fully experienced. To me it seemed outrageous, absurd, a cosmic error that our union which had touched and blessed so many lives should be so wastefully obliterated. Given our orientation toward responsibility, it was inevitable that I experienced the helplessness and outrage as anger at the 'tragic' flaw in Aldie's nature – his unrealized potential that made death the only viable alternative to a future half-life half lived.

Afterward I told Aldie what Joey and I had talked about, but it was not really necessary. Aldie already knew. He knew, even better than Joe and I, the reasons for our anger, feeling them as keenly. Thus, he could forgive us venting it to each other, knowing it would alleviate our pressure on him.

If Joey and I had not grappled with the force of our anger, I do not think Aldie could have died as quickly and as beautifully as he did. People who have witnessed many deaths and are sensitive to the process, report that the dying often feel they cannot go if someone they love is hanging on – needing them still. I believe that unrecognized, unresolved anger between the dying and loved ones can prolong the process in a similar way. Anger is as strong a bond as love. As Aldie was preparing to go, he knew my anger had been resolved, but he was not yet sure that Joey's had. In the days before Joe and Julie could get there, he kept asking, "Do you think Joey is still angry at me for dying?" By the time he arrived, Joey too could tell Aldie honestly that the anger was gone, releasing Aldie to proceed with what he had to do. No way in this world could Joey or I have pretended. Aldie would have known. Even, or especially, in a family climate of openness, it is hard to face and handle that component of love we call anger. I wonder how many deaths are unwittingly prolonged by loved ones holding on to their unsurrendered needs or their unresolved angers.

After my three days in Virginia and just before I left for the Keys, Aldie put the purpose of our parting into words. He held me close and we cried together. He said that we had to undergo 'husband and wife surgery'. He was so right. Surrender to the ultimate separation had to be done before death came, not during, not after.

I do not fully understand the alchemy of Aldie's mind during our ten days apart. What I do know is that when they were over he was ready to perform the act of dying victoriously. I think now that Aldie had already come to the surrender point while we were still in Virginia for Thanksgiving, for it was there that he had spoken of a time when one should "roll with the disease instead of fighting it." Joey and I, at least, were simply not ready to hear what he was really saying.

The time apart was good for Aldie. He started to work on the glossary again with characteristically intense, short bursts of energy. He rested a lot, went for short walks, drove up to the corner every day for breakfast at a cafe he loved. Claudia and Richard joined him every afternoon for the five o'clock meditation and helped with dinner. Pat, first Julie's friend, then ours when she came to live in the converted greenhouse attached to our 'compound', checked in with Aldie every day. Now an invaluable part of my life, she tells me sometimes about that week. Aldie seemed serene, "occupied, sometimes preoccupied, but easily communicative," she says. He spent one long afternoon with his 'mentor', a close professional friend with whom Aldie loved to exchange whimsies about the unscientific behavior of marine plants. Pat says it was wonderful to hear their laughter. I am sure Aldie knew it was farewell.

He turned to Pat another day as they watched a pair of cardinals who nest in our yard and said, "You know, there are some things I am going to miss." Looking back upon that afternoon, Pat thinks that by then Aldie was perfectly at peace with the knowledge of his death, yet his willingness to die was in no way a rejection of life. His acceptance of death seemed to bring a certainty that he would experience a conscious existence afterward. This had not been a matter of deep conviction for Aldie during his lifetime. But that afternoon Pat felt his certainty, and I heard it several times in comments he made during his dying time.

Another happening that week was the final flowering of love between Julie and Aldie. Aldie and I talked on the phone every afternoon I was in the Keys. One day was a particularly bad one for me. It was impossible for him not to have known, of course. After we hung up he called Julie to heal his distress by talking. This was a new experience for Julie. For the first time she felt that Aldie really needed her, that she could give him something no one else could. She recorded her feelings in the journal I asked her to write after Aldie's death.

> After that first call, we talked every night about everything, trivial and momentous. I had him recount his daily efforts on the glossary in detail, and describe what was going on in his body and how he felt about it. I asked him "why?" to everything and he never balked, always answering as best he could. It helped me to understand him and his thoughts as never before.
>
> During that week of phone calls I could tell Aldie was getting a little weaker each day, but he was not frightened. He was too tired, seen it all. His voice was amazingly strong, and I had the feeling that he was confident – more so than when we had seen him at Thanksgiving.
>
> Those phone calls were our farewell. I remember saying to Joe that if I never talked to him again it would be all right because now we were complete friends. We had absolutely touched each other as *equals!* I had the odd sensation that he finally knew that I cared for *him*, not just because of mother.

As Joe listened to Julie's half of these phone calls, he said he'd realized for the first time that "Julie and Aldie were separate from all the others in their love for one another." This theme, of relationships completing and fulfilling themselves, repeated itself over and over during the dying time. It began at the family reunion when Tip made his hard gift of truth and Aldie realized, with surprise, that Tip really loved him for himself. The same kind of realization had to come with Julie. Each relationship, each link in the family network, had its own time of resolution as the last remaining barriers were removed. This became even more apparent as Aldie went into the final transformation. Then he was able to touch every person with a magic love that was special and unique to them. This was to cause some anxieties and jealousies until people began to understand that indeed everyone had been special to him; everyone had been uniquely intimate with him; and the intimacy of each enhanced the union of all.

If my week in the Keys had no other purpose than providing the opportunity for Aldie and Julie to discover the completeness of their love for each other, it would have been worth it. Death weaves a complex web of interconnected transformations and different sorts of changes were going on with me as well. Aldie was very honest with me during our phone conversations, admitting that he felt much freer alone in the house. He knew then, as I knew by the end of the week, that the intensity of my desire to have him live put a burdensome pressure on him. This pressure had been useful until that time, supporting his will to live and his hope for a future. But as he approached the point of surrender, it became instead a hindrance. Our sons and daughters had been right, if premature, in knowing that we would have to be apart to fully accomplish our separate surrenders – his to death, mine to loss, and both to separation.

Surrender is hard work. The three days in Virginia had been my time of purging. The next seven were the time for letting go. During the week in the Keys I worked on the outline for my seminar as sporadically as Aldie was working on his glossary.

In between I prayed. I meditated. Unable to sleep I did yoga out under the trees at three o'clock in the morning. I read a stack of books, exploring useful concepts of death, resurrection, reincarnation, and the purposes of pain from a dozen different traditions. I was driven by the imperative of my search to record the process in a journal. Even now, when I reread what I wrote that week, I am astounded at the wild swings from wracking agony to flights of ectasy and back again. The journal records my letting go, little by little, as I came to face the separation, and searched for a sense of purpose in it, gathering the conceptual materials and the exhausting emotions from which the miracle of acceptance would emerge.

I suppose the key to our whole experience lies in that word "acceptance." Within the week Aldie was to make a crucial distinction between his own experience of acceptance and giving up—between surrender and resignation. Resignation, giving up, is passive. Acceptance, surrender, requires active participation—indeed, it is an act of creation. There is much talk about the importance of acceptance both to the dying and the bereaved, but very little about the mechanics of acquiring it. The mechanics include a great deal of pain, wild swings into despair, brief glimpses of joy, raging anger, and a torturous casting about for a way to explain to oneself why such a totally unacceptable event is happening. At the heart of acceptance is the search for meaning—or rather an act of creating meaning where none exists.

Some come to acceptance and peace by embracing a tradition which explains and gives meaning to pain and death. Others have to hammer it out for themselves, using bits and pieces from various traditions, creating their own system of explanation and meaning. For many in our Pebble People network it was the latter.

One of the keys to my eventual acceptance was a new view of Aldie that was dawning. As it turned out, a very similar realization was working its way to the surface of Aldie's mind, opening up his path to transformation. During those brief flights of vision and joy that punctuated the pain of that week, I was beginning to see that the very qualities in Aldie which I railed against were precisely those which had most benefited all of us. What I had seen as his 'tragic flaw' – his inability to fling himself into lifesaving self-fulfillment – was also at the root of his genius for loving. This reinterpretation of Aldie's 'weakness' began in several journal entries:

> I am beginning to see Aldie as having used his maximum energies in loving – as having in a real sense 'saved' the kids and me. Now that the task is almost complete, why should he need to go on? Would the transformation we have assumed to be necessary be consistent with the basic pattern of this life-form of his? Would it not require a change in the very qualities that made him able to love us so uncritically? Non-aggressiveness, passive withdrawal in the face of anger, refusal to express hostility. Even the too-vulnerable inability to resist the erosion of confidence under academic attack. His very inability to fight for himself is what saved all of us. His defenselessness created the love-strength in others. This is what made it possible for us to harness our love to the hard facts of family and parental life. Would the transformation necessary for him to be a 'non-cancer' sort of person produce an Aldie so different as to not be the same person who lifted us all to the heights of love?
>   I begin to see Aldie in a truly heroic light – pushed to maintain a life-form that he has used creatively but doesn't need any more. He has said so often in the last three years, "I know I am not using up all my energies." Is this an intuitive stretching ahead into the next growth phase for him? It might well require the death transition to free him from the shackles of this person pattern.

At the same time I could see why my drive to 'fix things' during our times of separateness had been so frustrated. The urge to 'fix things' psychologically and emotionally is commendable, but very much a part of our cultural assumption which tells us problems are to solve, not bear. I began to see that the characteristic in Aldie which had caused me so much pain—his refusal to look at or even remember our separateness—was probably the very mechanism that had kept our love infinitely resurrectable, clean-washed, and all new over and over again. A rather unrealistic Peter Pan approach. Some problems in a relationship can and should be 'fixed'—changed. But some arise from deep patterns that lie at the very heart of a person's uniqueness.

These problems cannot be 'fixed', no matter how deep the love, because it is the obverse side of these same characteristics that brings joy. After you have dug up all those psychological insights, or reached the highest moral stance, whichever you will, you are still left with a residue of pain-producing problems. Then is the time to leave both the psychological and the moralistic view of man behind and step forward into the spiritual dimension from which you can see both sides of the same quality.

At the beginning of our life together, Aldie and I used to laugh about him being 'Satan in tweeds'. He was so unwavering in his pursuit of satisfaction for deeply felt inner needs. While this freed him from ambivalence and gave him power, it often turned into undisciplined abandonment—like drinking to the point of blunting our fine-tuning to each other on which our lives depended.

Now as our life together was drawing to a close I could see how his satanic self was indeed divine, his Judas his Christ, his weaknesses his strengths, and his vices his virtues. This wholistic view of each other is what we had been groping for during the dialogue in Fort Worth in August. Now it had grown to become the ultimate perception of the wholeness in which life and death are but complimentary parts. When I could see these things, I was lifted up above the world of duality and felt an incredible sense of freedom and joy even in the face of death. The rhythm of peaks and valleys through which I had been swinging all week ended on a high as I drove home Tuesday, the week before Christmas.

Our being together had somehow changed. Suspended in closeness, there was an overwhelming feeling of joy and freedom. The question of success or failure seemed to take on a completely different meaning, as we had both finally come to accept Aldie's dying. Hope itself had been transformed. Life and living were no longer the criteria for victory. I knew that Aldie would die, that I would grieve and that there would be pain. The Pebble People network had generated a tremendous feeling of hope and certainty during the initial radiation period. At that time, with the success of Aldie's remission, my heart had exploded with gratitude and a powerful sense of triumph. Now, with the imminence of Aldie's death, my heart was filled in a new way. I was no longer hoping to alter or change the facts of his disease or of his death. Ironically, it is as though this was the change I had searched for at the ashram and with the second radiation period. This was the change I had not thought to hope for, yet it is what enabled us to transform both his living and his dying. Our training time was over and the test of our growing about to begin. Aldie and I cherished each moment of those two days alone before family and friends began to arrive to celebrate Christmas. We rested from our labors together and in love.

# The Dying

*"... bereavement is a universal and integral
part of our experience of love."*

C. S. Lewis

# Preparation

THE NIGHT JENNIFER came home for Christmas, Aldie noticed that his legs were a little wobbly. The next morning we went up to the corner cafe where he liked to eat breakfast and he asked me to drive. As we walked from the car to the restaurant he said in a rather surprised way, "You know, I think I'm going to take your arm and lean on you a little. I do feel uncertain on my legs."

Since October, he had lost weight, the pain was a constant companion, and he rested every afternoon; but otherwise he had not been disabled. While I was in the Keys he had noticed some swelling in the ankles and Kenneth had sent him to a local oncologist. Some tumors in the groin area were interfering with the circulation in his legs, and Aldie had made an appointment for the next Monday for us both to see the oncologist and hear what therapy program he had in mind.

While we were having breakfast that morning, we decided to stop on the way home at a medical supplies place a few blocks away and rent a walker. By that afternoon Aldie had fallen over twice with the walker. They were frightening falls. Neither of us could grasp the speed with which he was losing the use of his legs. I had to take the walker back the next morning, Friday, and trade it in for a wheelchair. Afraid to wait until Monday to find out what was going on, we called the doctor and made an appointment for that afternoon. By the time we were ready to go, Aldie could not even swing his legs over the edge of the bed to help us move him into the wheelchair. It took four of us, Jennifer, Pat from the greenhouse, Richard who came from work, and me to get him to the doctor's office.

The doctor said we should go straight from his office to the hospital for tests. He suspected a tumor on the spine, telling us that some were operable – not as a life-extension measure, but as an attempt to regain the use of his legs for whatever time Aldie had left. We refused (thinking the test could not start until Monday morning) and promised to come in on Sunday afternoon.

Later the doctor told us that he had urged the immediate trip to the hospital because he could arrange tests to start Saturday morning. There is no question in my mind that the doctor *did* tell us this, but we chose not to hear him! Neither of us could remember him saying the tests could start on Saturday.

I think now that we were beginning to experience a slight dissociation from 'ordinary reality'. At some level, we knew what was happening even before the tests, and we did not want the tumor to be operable. We knew that what we needed was time to be alone together and that the hospital was not the environment for what we had to say and experience in the next thirty-six hours. Also, I believe that Aldie was even then making the choice to terminate therapies and that our selective hearing of what the doctor was saying was a protection against being in a situation where surgery might have been recommended. As it turned out, if the specialists had seen Aldie that Saturday morning, we would have had to either fight off their pressure for surgery or go along with it and subject ourselves to conventional systems of life-extension. By somehow misunderstanding the doctor, we kept ourselves outside of the medical system until it was just barely too late to operate.

We went home from the doctor's office on Friday night and by Saturday morning, Aldie was paralyzed from the chest down. He still had sensation in his upper legs and torso, but was unable to move himself around in bed and could only with difficulty raise his head to eat or drink. By Saturday noon we had installed a hospital bed with all the gadgets that make it practical to care for a paralyzed patient, including an air mattress that undulates slightly, preventing bedsores. It is amazing how quickly one picks up bits of information about necessary equipment and how quickly rental services can deliver what you need.

After the flurry of activity, Aldie was resting in his new bed and I sat in a chair near the foot. The shock of what had happened in the last twenty-four hours suddenly hit me and I could feel a pressure rising inside me. It was a wholly irrational urge to DO something, to stop what was happening, I cannot remember what I said, but Aldie knew I was sliding back down into the pit I'd so recently thought forever left behind. It made him weary.

"I can't haul you out again, Bujie," he said. His eyes were so tired. I left him then to go hide in my office where I wept, shuddering and groaning, huddled in the armchair, curled up around the terrible pain in my chest and stomach. In spite of my week in the Keys when I had come to terms with letting Aldie go, the suddenness of the paralysis had knocked me off balance and I was newly terrified of the truth that had come too soon. No more was there that little scrap of hope that the transformation Aldie and I had worked so hard at all year would leave us on the same side of that last final canyon. Voices cried out to Aldie from inside me, desperately, hideously, calling to him to "CHANGE. Make yourself different! Do what you have to do to be different so that the cancer won't have to kill you. Don't leave me! I can't live without you. You can do it. I know you can. People can cheat death at the last minute!" The words were only in my head. The only sound in the room was a sort of choked gulping.

Jennifer found me there. With the wisdom of the ages she got me to speak it all out and was not afraid. It all spilled out, fears that were twenty years old – the fear that indeed the giving of ourselves wholly to each other with nothing left over even for God had been a sacrilege, leaving us totally vulnerable to each other's loss, bringing us truly to the brink of hell. But as the words came gasping and hiccuping from my chest, a pride welled up, and I found myself crying out "I'm proud! I'm proud! I'd do it again!" And some very quiet, wise part of myself way back inside was saying, "Of course, for that is how you give yourself completely to God. This dying is part of your love."

Then Jennifer began to comfort me by talking sure and strong. She started to say incredible things.

"Mother, it was not a sacrilege. Giving yourself to Daddy was giving yourself to Christ. Daddy *is* our Christ. He's just an ordinary human being, but he is *our* Christ. Don't you understand? And he will be with us after he dies just as Jesus came back to the people who loved *him*." At last the agony subsided and I could go back to the bedroom spent, weary, red-eyed, heavy – but not afraid. The fullness of acceptance was not quite complete, but I was no longer crippled by resistance.

It was Ric, during a phone call later that afternoon, who put the finishing touches on my long labor of letting go. Somehow he found the words that made me see once and for all that I had to "let Aldie be Aldie, even if this included his dying." The surrender that had begun in the Keys finally slipped into place as a permanent part of my psychic pattern.

That night, really early Sunday morning, Aldie wasn't sleeping very well, nor was I. About two o'clock Aldie roused me. He started to talk and must have gone on for two hours. Such things were said! Such gates swung open on silent hinges! The next morning neither of us could remember exactly what we had said. Awareness and knowledge and insights fell like rain and it was irrelevant whose lips spoke them. After the miracle of sharing, we slept again fitfully until about six, when I got a pencil and paper and we tried to reconstruct what it was we had talked about during the night. We couldn't remember it all, but I have enough of Aldie's words to allow his transformation to shine through.

Aldie had started by saying, "Our love had no beginning and it will have no end. Our working side by side these last eighteen years has been simply part of an ongoing thing."

I told him I thought his greatest gift was that he created strength in others. He said, "I'd like that as my epitaph." We both laughed, for people who want their ashes sprinkled on a coral reef don't have epitaphs.

Then Aldie said, "I cannot really desire release unless I know that you will be all right."

As he said that, something slid into place in my heart, and I said with surprise, "How strange! The only way I could survive would be to know that you want to be released!" We looked at each other for a moment, realizing we had just given each other the one thing each of us needed. We had created in one another the strength neither could have gained alone.

Then we talked for a long time about the structure of our lives together—the outward forms through which we had channeled the energies of love. Marriage to us was simply a structure, not the strength of the love. It did provide a channel through which the energy of the love could work in other people's lives. We had never been able to find a structure for the spiritual part of ourselves, nor rituals to express feelings and beliefs about the purpose and meaning of life. Aldie had always been wary of such structures. Neither of us could find satisfaction in the church even after years of working within it, but we had never found a substitute. The closest we ever came to a structure was our 'flow-through' house where kin and non-kin were always welcome to absorb and share love. The closest we ever came to a formal ritual in our lives was the Pebble People meditation. Yet, even that we chose to limit to a five-week period, wary of institutionalizing our ritual of love. We did not want to build a cathedral out of pebbles.

That last night together we talked about the spiritual dangers of remaining too far outside conventional structures and shared belief systems. "Your sense of purpose," Aldie said, "has made you yearn for a structure. You were always going to build one. In some ways you are telling me things now I've never heard before. For many years I felt structure as a threat. My nature had an iconoclastic side to it. From the start, from early teen age, I railed out against structure and convention in my town, my own family. Those structures represented great cruelties. Now I've come around to view it as a necessary thing. A life does need structure. My resistance to all the belief systems, the disciplines we've tried this year—I regret it, but not much.

"I look upon my life as a success," he continued, "a happy thing with no beginning and no end. It's been a delight! Yes I've had unhappy times but I could hide them and live on the joys. I don't feel I've ever been cheated in my life. I think that's a nice thing to be able to say."

"Then why not go on with it?" I asked.

"Why?" This exchange was so quick and so spontaneous that we both burst out laughing. Aldie went on: "Going on requires an extraordinary fight—against the disease. I've never been a fighter, at least for myself. I always fight for someone else. I fought for you and I fought for the kids. I fought to win you. I'm highly motivated by another person.

"And all year long," I said, "we have been trying to make you fight for yourself."

"Yes. And the kids have been critical because I wouldn't fight. But I did fight for them. I fought to win their love. This just happens to be part of my psychological make up. If I hadn't had this particular psychological make up I don't think I'd ever have worked so hard for the children. My hang-ups made things difficult but they supplied a force, a driving force. My particular hang-ups have been useful! People have often said that I had peculiar ways of doing things. I feel now that my particular psychological make up has been a burden to me and I find it gives me a sense of freedom and release to be laying it aside. I bear it no malice now. I feel now that I can lay it aside. It's taken a long time and a lot of pain to get here – to the willingness to surrender. But I didn't work at it. It just came. I just bore the pain. The thing that amazes me is my lack of argument with my life."

"How can you feel such satisfaction with your life and at the same time be so willing to leave it?" I asked. "I should think you'd want to hang on to such a satisfying life."

"The only things you are not willing to leave behind," he answered, "are things you haven't experienced. If I felt cheated, I couldn't release, let go. I never did ask to die. But I have a far greater willingness. I voiced this before Chicago, the need to come to grips with the fear of death and a need to come to grips with surrender. The sense of release is tied up in a complex set of thoughts not the least of which is my contentment with my life. I am not asking out. Surrender and giving up are different. I don't *desire* to die. I don't *want* to die. It hurts me when people say that. What I desire is making my peace. There is a difference between desiring death and accepting it. I accept it.

"I said I feel my psychological make up has been a burden. What I can't understand is why I can feel this without a concurrent sense of guilt. My psychological make up has brought a lot of pain to other people. I am seeing this now, maybe for the first time. But it's coming without guilt. There's nothing to change. What's the point? People who know me and love me will understand. Particularly if they know I feel the full weight of my responsibility in this – in having hurt them. But it's not a hang-up for me to work out. It's just something for others to understand as part of me. Last night when I realized my particular framework had been a burden, I also realized I could let it go. The prospect of death spurs the sense of letting go. Maybe I could have come to it without illness, but dying speeds up these processes. Dying speeds up surrender and the transformation process."

That night brought a sense of perfect communion — of having resolved all the unfinished business between us. Tradition would name it 'repentance' and 'forgiveness'. Witnessing Aldie's remarkable insights into himself and his complete self-acceptance had a strange, freeing effect on me. It made me know that I, too, bear the burden of a particular psychological make up and that, while certain emphases can be changed by self-awareness, the basic pattern is neither alterable nor eternal. It is something to be worn like a partly-beautiful, partly-ugly garment — to be accepted while I wear it, and set aside with relief when the time comes. Knowing this to be true of both Aldie and me, I can no longer experience the slightest twinge of anger. Nor can I experience that special sort of torment that comes from thinking "if only . . . ." "If only I had been more able to accept his drinking. If only I had been able to understand his withdrawals." For of course Aldie felt the same way about his inadequacies, and, as he was able to accept his own, he could forgive mine, counting on me to do the same. The quality of him that night, and for the two weeks between then and his death, was of such a clear-seeing, light-infused nature that it leaves no doubt in my mind that at the last a true divinity came into our lives. It permeated every fibre of our beings. Death could no more extract it than you can dig stain out of a piece of wood that has been soaked in it.

After this moment in time, things went so very quickly. It was as if that last night the stars paused in their circling flight, waiting for us to surrender up each other, and then rushed on to make up for lost time. By eleven o'clock that Sunday morning the paralysis had crept up and all sensation as well as motor activity was going. We were due at the hospital that evening, but Aldie had me make arrangements for the ambulance at noon. He called the oncologist and found that the two specialists, a surgeon and a neurologist, who were to examine him just happened to be at the hospital. Within the hour he was undergoing a series of tests and consultations.

I have been asked since if we weren't terrified by the swiftness of the paralysis. The falls on Thursday, of course had been very frightening. But I think both of us had fully internalized Aldie's earlier insight—"we must never, never again mistake the physical effects for the real disease. The real struggle is in the mind." As the paralysis progressed, our attention was upon our inner mobilizing. We knew the dying was upon us. It had come faster than we had expected, but neither of us were fooled by the chimera of time, as if a few weeks more made a difference. It was a matter of recognizing the right moment to terminate all therapies and "let the cancer take its course" as Aldie said it. He had called Carl Simonton just before we left for the hospital to ask if he believed in such a point and just when he thought it should come. Carl's warmth and love made tears flow down Aldie's cheeks. Carl said he thought every family had to find that point for itself. Aldie wanted all the information he could get about where the tumors were and what organs they were affecting before he made his final decision. Three days in the hospital were the price of this information.

Once all the wheels were in motion, we both moved with complete confidence and a strange pride toward our awesome destination. The early Sunday morning communion had initiated a state of heightened awareness—a two-dimensional consciousness which focused all our energies, and in which irrelevancies simply disappeared. I found myself operating with incredible efficiency in the external world. Strength just poured through with no effort or awareness of accomplishment. Sitting in the emergency waiting room as the tests began, I felt a peculiar kind of serenity, as if something had been settled and I was free to move absolutely in any direction necessary. When the neurologist and the surgeon called me for a conference in the hallway (always in the hallway!) I could see their decision-struggle. Depending upon the exact time the day before the paralysis had crept to such and such a point, they would recommend for or against surgery. I remember feeling sorry for them. I tried to take the burden of decision upon myself and to help them feel good about the fact that it was too late to operate. I wished I could have shared with them the beauty that was happening.

When Aldie was settled in a room, we talked about alerting the network again, asking them to pour their energies into what we called a 'quick release'. Aldie decided to wait until the next morning for the liver scan which would indicate the extent of organ involvement. The doctors had made it clear that the spinal tumors would not bring death, only keep him paralyzed for his remaining time – which they guessed at maybe three months. The spread of cancer to a vital organ, though, could shorten that time.

That afternoon Aldie began to take charge with an energy I had not seen for weeks. The first thing he did was to send me out for cigarettes! The behavioral changes that were no longer relevant were shucked off like an old coat. Then he began to tick off items for me to remember – things like which account to draw upon for certain expenses, and which broker to call upon if I decided to sell the boat. He specifically warned me that I would be tempted to 'pull in my horns', and get uptight about money, and think about selling the house. He told me to resist this temptation and that to stay happy I had to 'stay expansive'. He had always been the guardian of the free-flowing, gear-shifting nature of our lives and he knew I would have to find ways to do this for myself. He was so right! The temptation did come and it had very little to do with financial reality. It was more of a security move, an attempt to somehow make my life smaller and more controllable. That would have been the worst thing for me to do. 'Getting on top of things' is a very uncreative motivation for me. It closes out unpredictable options.

Then Aldie astonished me by saying firmly, "Now, Ginnie, I want you to know you are free to marry again." I answered immediately that I could not imagine such a thing, and yet a peculiar sense of freedom was born at that moment. It was as if he were making a gift of me to myself. In the months since, I have lost that vision of wholeness and freedom, but I still remember the lightness and joy, the overwhelming love for Aldie that grew inside me all during the afternoon and evening until I could not sleep that night for the love that was flowing into me from, and out from me to, the whole universe! When the night nurse shone her flashlight into my eyes at the 3 AM check, I was even glad. Her's was another human hand to touch with all that love. Maybe someday I will understand the true nature of the gift Aldie gave me through that quite unremarkable sentence.

The next morning the liver scan showed some involvement, but not enough to suggest a short terminal phase. We were warned that it could last as long as three months and a combined radiation-chemotherapy program was suggested. I am still not really sure just what the rationale of this was. The paralysis was considered irreversible and it is difficult to imagine that anyone would think of radiation and chemotherapy as making a patient more 'comfortable'. Maybe life-extension technologies are sometimes a concerned doctor's equivalent of that desperate cry to "DO something! CHANGE something!" that tore through me just the day before. Putting forth his predictable arguments for the therapy that morning, the oncologist said, "Of course, you realize that I have to come down on the side of life." I wish now that one of us had been quick enough to say, "So do we, but we spell it with a capital 'L'."

Aldie made his decision to refuse further treatment

while I was off arranging for money to pay the hospital bills. I am glad he did it without any more discussion between us. I felt it meant he was sure of both himself and me and that he was entirely unambiguous about his surrender. I have always believed that it is an underlying ambiguity in accepting death that sets up the conditions for a prolonged 'hanging on'.

That night I made the few phone calls that would alert the family and close network to start the five o'clock meditations again, this time with a quick release as the purpose. My thoughts flew to all of the Pebble People and the healing power that had flowed through them a year before. If the power of love could facilitate physical healing, why could it not also facilitate the 'wholing' we call death. I was absolutely certain that their energies would help Aldie free himself from a lingering death. There was never any doubt in my mind that it would be only two or three weeks at most.

After Aldie's decision to refuse further therapy he and Ric had a phone conversation which was their own very special farewell. Ric had been undecided about whether or not he wanted to fly down. He no longer felt the need as the phone communication with Aldie fulfilled their relationship, just as Julie had completed her relationship with Aldie in their phone conversations while I was in the Keys.

"Aldie said that he wasn't giving up," Ric told me later, "but that he was going to let happen what would happen, and that he had made peace with his maker like Molli had said. I got the feeling that he'd had some kind of religious experience and was totally at peace. It was in his tone of voice – he was completely at ease. An awful burden had been taken off him. He said he had been afraid of leaving you, not knowing if you could handle it alone. But now he was relieved, and didn't feel he had to continue to fight. After the reunion at Madeline Island, I felt that no way could he feel easy until he had come to peace. That is pretty much what he said on the phone and that gave me what I needed. That's all I wanted Aldie to do. A lot wasn't said between us, but it didn't need saying."

Connie, who was in the hospital room during that call, remembered how Aldie looked. "He was just beaming and started to cry because he felt so good about it."

The hospital staff, during the three days Aldie was there, was absolutely fantastic. All of the nurses on all three shifts were fully supportive of our decision to take Aldie home to die. They taught me things I needed to know. They even encouraged me to give him his Demerol shots under their supervision so I could gain confidence in something I had never done before and was nervous about. They spent time explaining dosages in detail, how to draw the right amount out of the container, how to figure the per- cent of the potentiating drug that is given with Demerol, just how to pull the plunger back slightly to be sure the needle has not hit a vein. They told me stories about their first 'shot' experiences to make me laugh and relax. They let me help with all of the tasks including enemas and explained how to keep records of the liquid intake so I could judge a satisfactory urine output in the catheter bag. The first night one of the nurses ordered a cot for me to sleep on without my even having to ask for it.

I think a family that has made a decision for a home death, and expresses no ambiguity about the decision, is most likely to elicit positive response from medical personnel. Our determination and the fact that we'd made practical arrangements well in advance increased their trust in us, freeing them to give us the help we needed. They knew that we had discussed a home death with our family doctor weeks before and that we had already talked with a mortuary to arrange for the very simple services we would need from them— pick up of the body after death, cold storage for the required three days, and simple cremation.

Some of the nurses seemed a bit nonplussed that we had already made these arrangements and could discuss them so casually. In retrospect it rather surprises me too. In the fall, when we had done it, though, it seemed a necessary part of our commitment to "participating in our own death process." While we were discussing our fears, Aldie's of death and mine of separation, I had realized that one real source of anxiety for me was the uncertainty about practical details. Would we have to fight with the doctor to let Aldie die at home? We had already decided we both wanted to be cremated and scattered on coral reefs. Would I have to argue with some mortician about refusing to buy a casket? Such puny details, but of such is a sleepless night born! So we had asked Ken if he would cooperate in a home death, and, of course, he would as he had done for others. Then Aldie had suggested I call a mortuary whose ad for a 'rock bottom' priced cremation he had seen in the paper. I felt weird making the call, so Aldie looked up the number and sat in a chair behind me while I called. It is really surprising how terribly unimportant these 'traumatic' details become if they are decided and disposed of before the real trauma begins.

It was important that the hospital nurses supported our decision, not only because of what they taught me, but because their confidence that I could do it gave me confidence in myself. After all the emotional upheavals that had led to our decision and after all the practical arrangements we had made, I still felt moments of anxiety about taking the responsibility for Aldie's care when he was so physically helpless and would become more so. The hospital nurses dispelled any lingering doubts I had about a terminal patient getting better care in a hospital. They assured me that the skills necessary for our purposes were relatively few and easily learned, reminding me that part-time nursing care at home was available if we needed it. They said that no matter how much hospital nurses care, they can never offer the entirely personalized services that willing family members can provide.

I could see for myself that some of the pain-producing

practices that are standard in a hospital simply needn't be done at home. In a hospital a paralyzed patient is turned regularly, partly to keep lungs from filling up. If they do fill up they are suctioned to help the patient breathe. Both processes can be very painful. At home neither needs to be done. Lungs full of fluid just make breathing harder. That didn't hurt Aldie half as much as turning him did. And if you don't suction, the patient simply dies faster — of pneumonia, the 'kindly killer' as Aldie used to call it — instead of waiting a few more weeks for the cancer to hit some vital organ. When a patient can no longer eat or doesn't want to, the hospital feeds him through tubes. At home the lack of nourishment contributes to the process of vital organ shutdown.

We brought Aldie home in an ambulance on the afternoon of Christmas Eve. At this point there were four of us to take care of him: Connie, who had arrived while Aldie was in the hospital; Jennifer, who had decided that Aldie's impending death should not prevent her friend Matt's Christmas visit as Matt was dear to her and she wanted him to meet Aldie; Matt whom I admire for having the courage to come; and myself.

The 'ancillary staff', people who filled in neglected household tasks, consisted at this time of Pat and Suzanna. Suzanna lives in an apartment attached to the house, and hovers around the outside of our lives like a lovely little melody heard only in snatches. Claudia and Richard lived about fifteen minutes away and were in and out of the house every day except for a week which they spent with their respective parents in other parts of the country. We had had two days to ready the house for its new role, getting in medical supplies and filling the sheaf of prescriptions ordered by our doctor.

Connie, arriving in the middle of it, had to adjust to the new pressures quickly. She is our psychic one — always warned ahead of time in remarkable dreams (which she never believes until the event occurs), and sometimes able to experience in her own body the pain of others. She and Aldie had always communicated through a method they called the 'vibes'. Connie has a kind of strength that even she doesn't understand. On the day of her arrival, she wrote in her journal:

> A heavy day! The minute I got there, a ton of things to be done. Dad does look good. His eyes twinkle and are peaceful, when not intent on alleviating pain. Mom's pretty strong and together but needs occasional support—to be expected. She seems to be tunnel-visioned right now, getting Daddy home and taking care of him. Which is what needs to be done. I feel somewhat overwhelmed now, having made some phone calls delivering the news. Joe and Julie were shocked. It came so fast and they're unprepared. Julie cried. I was almost jealous that she could react so sensitively, so quickly. I wonder about me sometimes. Am I made of nails and have no feelings? Where is the heaviness of sorrow I expected? What's going on inside me? I don't feel sad about losing Aldie—at least not yet. I just want it over for him. I worry that somehow I failed him—not loved him enough or showed him in serious ways. Am I *really* facing it? I have all these questions because what everyone calls 'strength' in me just keeps carrying me on. Am I missing the whole thing? I don't know. I trust my psyche is doing what is best for me. It warns me in my dreams and I get a sense of elation at the thought of Aldie's death.
>
> God, please allow Aldie to go quickly, with as little pain as possible. Joey needs to be here. Let the light filter out easily. Carry his soul, letting him rest.

Joe and Julie were to leave for Ireland to spend Christmas with friends the very day Aldie's paralysis set in. By the time we realized what was happening, they were in the air. Aldie had been adamant about their going, knowing what it meant to them. They were making a decision about a permanent move. Trusting Aldie to let them share in his death, they were unprepared when it began while they were so far away. Julie wrote:

> I wasn't prepared for what Connie said on the phone. Poor dear, she was exhausted. Daddy was in the hospital, this and this is going on in his body, hope for a swift death.

It was too abrupt. We had left him well. We had left him
Aldie. We had left him ours. And now suddenly he wanted a
swift death. It was a passage of too many experiences that
we had missed — it crossed too many logical steps — we were
not ready for this and we were too far away. Connie said
Aldie wanted us to stay. We knew there was really nothing
else we could do. There were no earlier flights back.

The wise thing asked to speak to Joey — she said she
wanted to explain to him too. He was very quiet and calm.
We went back upstairs with the whole household knowing
the problem. Gail held me. The tears were coursing down
our common cheek. Joe turned to a fury and began to yell
and cry. He pounded the walls with his fist. I remember
wondering what we were going to do if he punched a hole
in the plaster, who would fix it and how much it would cost.

# First Plateau

THE FIRST FIVE DAYS after we brought Aldie home from the hospital I call the first plateau. It was the first of two periods of relatively stable condition, each quite different from the other, and both quite different from the normal mental-emotional state in which he left the hospital.

There had been a lot of pain in his right arm and across his shoulders in the hospital because of the tests and the necessity of moving him. By the time he was settled in at home Christmas Eve, he was suffering greatly. I was giving him Demerol shots and some other medication the doctor wanted to try which didn't work. At midnight he finally went to sleep. I thought how symbolic it was, knowing they would be singing *Silent Night* with the creche lights on in the churches we had once loved. At three o'clock in the morning he was awake. I asked him how it was going and he said, "You know, the pain is almost gone."

It was really remarkable. From that time on for a whole week he was relatively pain free. He didn't need the Demerol or the heavy codein drug he had been using all fall. He was able to control the pain with a level of medication that hadn't helped him since August. A qualitative change in his state of consciousness occurred at the same time. He tired more easily than he had in the hospital, but it wasn't just that. He was perfectly capable of rational exchange, but it was as if his mind were one step removed. Curiously, as he moved further and further away from normal, rational thought processes, his control over dying seemed to increase.

Always having been knowledgeable about chemistry and pharmaceuticals, Aldie had worked with Ken in setting up our rather extensive medicine kits for the summer cruises when we were far away from medical help for weeks at a time. So it was not surprising that he was able to select the type and amount of medication that best fit his needs. What amazed us was the complexity of the relationship between the medication and the psychic states he was experiencing. It seemed as if he were steering a careful course, trying to maintain a balance between the amount of pain he was willing to tolerate and his need for alertness and the ability to communicate.

Starting with his decision in the hospital, it seemed to us that he was moving increasingly into a leadership role with the rest of us working to facilitate his decisions. Our care for him was not so much a responsibility for a dependent person as an attempt to understand and serve a person who knew what he was doing and where he was going but needed help in getting there. It seems to me that it is this quality of the death process that can be enhanced by a home, rather than a hospital, death. I cannot believe that Aldie was unique in his capacity to control his death experience. It seems more logical to assume that death, squarely faced, confers a knowledge beyond that which we can gain rationally and that this knowledge on the part of any dying person should be respected, encouraged, and implemented.

This part of our experience was especially important because of Aldie's past fears. When he fully recognized his fear of death in August and began to deal with it, he realized that he didn't fear death itself as much as the "humiliation and passivity of a cancer death." Passivity in his own nature was something Aldie fought all his life, and it seemed as if the death toward which he was moving was the ultimate in humiliating dependency—that the

part of his psychological make up he liked least was going
to be most fully expressed. Yet the process of death, when
it began in earnest, was quite the opposite. As he became
more and more dependent upon our physical care, his
stature as leader increased.

Christmas morning was a quiet ceremony. No one had
spent much time on presents, and what Christmas we had
was mostly an exchange of things gotten together before
the sudden paralysis. His speech not yet impaired, Aldie
communicated naturally during the Christmas ritual,
though there was a quiet, almost distracted quality. None
of us were really into Christmas, and curiously, no one
really minded all that much. It was as if all of us – Connie, Jennifer, Matt, Aldie, and I – were going through the
motions together as a way to pass the time until we could
get to some really important activity.

Either Christmas afternoon or the next day I became
aware that the frequent periods of rest Aldie took were not
just sleep. It was as if he were going into other spaces in
his head. He would always respond if one of us spoke to
him, but we had the impression that he was not waking
from sleep as much as making an effort to come back from
somewhere else. I asked him what was happening in those
other spaces.

He said "I used to be so afraid of the humiliation and the
passivity and, now that it is upon me, I realize my fears
were illusory. In those spaces I am able to lay aside the
burden of my ego, and that is a very nice feeling."

By the end of Christmas week, Ed and Jane, Aldie's
brother and sister-in-law, had arrived. Aldie's daughter
Meredith, my stepdaughter, who had stayed with us many
times over the years and whom I counted as one of my most
beloved friends, had arrived as well. Merdi stayed in the
makeshift bedroom that had been my office, while Ed and
Jane settled themselves in a nearby motel. I did not ask
specific people to come. As always our doors were open to
anyone, and by the same hidden chemistry that had ruled

our lives in the past, the right combination of people sorted themselves out of our network and simply arrived. The people who did not come were no less beloved or loving. Each found his or her own way into their proper role for the dying.

During the first plateau, Aldie spoke many times about how satisfied he was with his life. He kept saying over and over, "I just can't believe how content I am with my life—how very happy and fulfilling it has been." He would say it with a sort of wonderment, as if in piecing it all together he had discovered something. Needless to say, this discovery was very gratifying to those around him who had shared his life.

His interactions with us were very short and very intense. He often referred to some past event, but never in a hallucinatory way that first week. It was always something specifically related to the person he was talking with, some very meaningful experience he had shared with that particular person. It was a sort of shared life review—with Ed there were memories of their boyhood in the Poconos; with Jane, incidents from the adolescence the three of them had shared (He shocked her once by calling from the bedroom, "Jane, have you been properly naughty lately?); with Merdi and Connie and Jennifer he talked about childhood events special to each of them. He spoke of how it would be after he died. Jennifer told him to be sure "not to look back once you've crossed the line, but just to keep going." With the perspective of her experiences since, she says she'd say it differently: "Once you're comfortable there, look back." Connie, who is into Tibetan Buddhism, asked him to "go with the clear light." Once he told Connie he was afraid that he would be able to see and hear all of us but we might not be able to see and hear him.

His exchanges with me consisted almost entirely of assurances of love, sometimes almost wordless, sometimes using the little formulas that husbands and wives evolve over the years:

"Who do you love?"

"Alden Eaton Hine."

"*That's* the right answer!"

Or a sudden "You're loved!" as I passed the bed when I thought he was asleep.

One of the things that surprised and delighted us was the marvelous humor that permeated our days. The whimsical phrase or flight of fancy that had been Aldie's most beloved trait, so buried under pain in the last months, seemed to burst forth during this week to catch all of us in unexpected moments of laughter.

Our days began to structure themselves during the first plateau. While I knew myself to be cast in a central role, I did no organizing and very little decision-making, except with respect to the nursing-care tasks. People seemed to sort themselves into the nursing staff and the household support group. Jane became orange-juice queen, and every morning about 9:30 the back door would slide open and the juicer would begin to whirr. Aldie wanted only liquids and orange juice was his favorite. Ed fell into the Mr. Fixit role which had not been properly filled for several months. In the end, as more and more people came and each found his role, we had eight doing round-the-clock nursing, and ten cooking, cleaning, shopping, washing endless loads of laundry, doing yard work, and loving up the jungle on the patio until it looked like a picture in *House and Gardens*.

Our little fiction of the vice-presidents came into being at this time. Whenever my eyes fell upon a task that needed doing, I appointed the person nearest as Vice-President in Charge of it. Soon others were appointing vice-presidents and still others appointed themselves. At one point we even had a Vice-President in Charge of Sewing Up the Tear in the Couch Cover—a tear that had been there for three years. I was the only one who didn't carry the distinction of wearing at least four vice-presidential hats. The game of having to seek out other vice-presidents whose jurisdictions overlapped one's own helped to knit a very disparate collection of people into a cooperating unit. Everyone who participated in Aldie's death experience, including Aldie and me, met at least three of the others for the first time. Some were complete strangers to most of the rest.

Ken Swords called every day even though he was supposed to be on vacation. I am sure he would have come to the house had we needed him, but we didn't really need more than the confidence that he knew how we were doing. He had put me in touch with a nursing service which agreed to send a registered nurse in two weeks to change the catheter that had been inserted in the hospital, as the paralysis had made it impossible for the bladder to empty naturally. Ken also suggested that I call the American Cancer Society. To my great surprise and eternal gratitude, they arranged for a practical nurse to come three afternoons a week at no charge!

She was a storybook nurse, large of frame, exuberant of nature, and totally competent at the bedside where she exuded professional heartiness. Her major task was directing baths and bed changes, as it took four pairs of hands to move Aldie that much—a very painful process. She taught us how to fit a draw sheet as tight as a trampoline, how to move him up and down in bed using the draw-sheet 'hammock', and how to massage him with the least amount of disturbance. She had creams that disposed of bedsores in three days. She even added a few tricks to those I had learned from the hospital therapist about exercising Aldie's paralyzed legs several times a day.

As it turned out, we didn't really need her for all of the hours scheduled, but we could not have managed without her gifts of information. We realized that we didn't know how to gauge the nearness of death nor exactly what would happen. I had only witnessed one death, my father's from a stroke. The others had had no experience. I had marveled at how simply my father's death had occurred. He just breathed out one time and didn't breathe in again.

I knew it was not always that way, though. So Connie and Merdi and I spent a couple of afternoons talking about it with the nurse. We learned about signs of the approaching end – irregular pulse, a stronger odor than we already knew, eyes that are filmed over and will not shut all the way, often a special sort of sweat on the skin, and a certain breathing pattern of which I have forgotten the technical term but will never forget the rhythm.

We also learned that several things can happen at the moment of death and that precautionary measures can be taken. The sphincters can relax, releasing the contents of the bowels. On occasion, when the lungs have filled up, the final expiration can be accompanied by a surprisingly forceful expulsion of fluids and blood. We followed her advice and kept a towel or a plastic pad near the head of the bed to put over the face if necessary.

None of these things occurred, but all of us were grateful we knew about them and could have experienced them without shock or surprise. Merdi, Connie, and I digested all of this information slowly, examining the feelings that went with it, and wondering if we should tell the others, especially Jennifer who was only seventeen. We discovered that knowing all of this gave us a remarkable sense of preparedness and competence. It did not take long to figure out that withholding information would rob Jennifer and the others of their opportunity to feel the same. It would have been cruel to take a chance on someone's being unpleasantly shocked at the very end. So the information flowed out. Jennifer especially made me feel chagrined at even having thought to protect her. She hugged me fondly, even a bit patronizingly, and said she had sort of suspected such things. From then on I never worried about her participation in the whole nursing-care program. Several times she helped with the three-person task of cleaning up after a bowel movement. I realize now how we would have cheated her had we succumbed to a false sense of decency. The burden of grief has been easier to bear because we worked so hard. The physical labor of Aldie's care seemed to cleanse us of lingering guilts that so often plague the bereaved.

One of the most amazing things about the physiological aspect of the dying process was our experience with smells. Cancer is supposed to smell very bad. Nurses have told me that you can smell some terminal cancer patients all the way down the hall. We knew Aldie had a special smell. All during the previous year he had used it as his own indicator of when his immune system was working overtime in destroying and disposing of cancer cells. He had smelled it long before I could – during the first radiation series and again starting halfway through the second in October. We both rather liked the smell, though it was very faint. It was different from any other smell I have ever experienced – slightly sweet but not sickly. By the time Aldie was moving into the final stages, it had become very strong, and there was no question but that it was the smell of death. Everyone who came into the house recognized it. But it was not a bad smell to us. In fact we liked it! Even now, Jennifer sometimes smells it and says, "I know that Daddy is near me when I smell that beautiful smell." The conventional reality is that terminal cancer patients smell bad. Our reality was simply different. A folie à deux for eighteen people? Perhaps. If so, should we not explore more seriously the possibility of two or three or eighteen gathered together in love being able to change the 'reality' of death?

All during the five days of the first plateau, Aldie spent more and more time within himself, moving through many different states of consciousness. He moved into spaces where there was no humiliation, no helplessness, no ego, and no burden of lifelong psychological conflict. He seemed to fluctuate at will between interacting with us and going into these spaces. Often when there was a bowel movement to clean up or when we had to roll him painfully over for a shot, I noticed that he seemed to slip deliberately into another world. His eyes would become gray and slightly closed. He would go where no indignity could reach him. And, in doing so, he conferred dignity upon his broken body and upon us as we cared for it.

The last day of the first plateau, which was also the last day that Aldie could talk easily, was the day that our lovely RN came to fill out the endless forms that were required for her to come a week later and change the catheter. She arrived while I was out doing some errands and I returned to find her sitting by Aldie's bed, the irrelevancy of the forms forgotten on her lap. He must have been able to communicate to her some of the wonder of his experience for she stayed long after she was supposed to have been on her way. When Aldie tired, she joined us at the counter for tea, allowing us to fall in love with her English accent and giving us the gift of her clear appreciation for this dying-at-home.

There was an almost house party atmosphere, which must have seemed attractive (or obscene, depending upon one's view) to outsiders who came into the house during this time. Food was constantly being prepared and enjoyed. Clusters of two or three people were continually forming and reforming—at the counter, in the living room, on the patio, or in the yard—sharing incidents that occurred at the bedside, meeting someone for the first time and getting to know them, engaging in a 'heavy rap', or just sitting quietly smoking together. People joined in the five o'clock meditation or not as they were moved. The fellowship hour that followed was always well attended, and dinner was a fresh miracle to me every night. I never could figure out how it got there.

The bedroom where Aldie lay opens with double doors onto the living room which is separated from the kitchen only by the counter. He seemed comfortable being near, but just outside of, the main currents of movement through the house. He displayed a remarkable ability either to hear what was being said or to sense what was going on in the house even when he appeared to be asleep or in his other spaces. Once, toward the very end after Joe and Julie had come, Julie realized we had run out of milk and decided to run to the store. Aldie was sleeping and Joe was on watch. Julie tiptoed in and whispered, "Joe, is there anything you want at the store?" She says that Aldie's eyes popped open and he whispered back, "Don't forget the milk," Julie stared at him and then at Joe and said to Aldie, "How did you know we were out of milk?" He just shrugged his shoulders and smiled. "He knows everything that is going on," she commented in her journal. "He is still in control."

Sometimes Aldie's awareness seemed to span time. Once he asked me if he hadn't heard "Mark and Gary out there." I didn't know who he was talking about because both were ex-boyfriends of Connie's who had not been around for many months. I mentally wrote his question off as 'hallucination'. The next day both Mark and Gary appeared separately and entirely unexpectedly at the back door!

Aldie's seeming ability to span time was accompanied by the beginning of an almost symbolic perception of things. One day when our practical nurse had arrived, but before she came into Aldie's room, he asked Connie and Merdi if the nurse had two faces. His question was serious, asked with a puzzled frown. He said, "Maybe I was a bit spacey the last time she was here, but didn't she have another face she put on like a mask?"

It was impossible not to agree with him, for she did indeed shift gears as she approached the bedroom. Her manner as she discussed the practicalities with us in the living room was quite different from that she used in talking with Aldie in the bedroom. In no way was she hypocritical. It was simply that she was using two aspects of her nature. Aldie, whose perceptive antennae extended far beyond his field of vision or normal hearing by then, picked up on both of them and experienced them symbolically.

He also seemed able to offer a nonverbal solace to those

who just sat quietly beside his bed—as if his dying was a solvent for their angers, their griefs, their jealousies, and tensions. Pat was one of these. She was devoted to Aldie and was having a very hard time with her anger at the beginning. Unlike Joey and me, she did not experience it as anger at Aldie for failing her or leaving her.

"There was no one to direct my anger at," she said. "It was more like just shaking my fist at the sky. I was angry because if there was anyone in the world who shouldn't die, it would be Aldie. Aldie was exactly what the world needs more of. It seemed to me such a *waste!* But mostly I wasn't ready for Aldie to die. I wasn't ready to lose access to him."

She had come into the house the week before, the day we got the wheelchair, and saw him fall as we tried to shift him from the chair to the bed. Without telling us she was there she ran back to the greenhouse with her mind "screaming No! No!" She had not been able to come back into the house again until she felt she could get the terrible rage under control. When she finally did come, during the first plateau, I saw her go into the bedroom and leave again a moment later. I could tell something was the matter as I watched her quickly cross to the patio door, and I ran to catch up with her outside.

Bursting into tears, she said, "I couldn't stay! It still makes me so angry!" I held her, trying to comfort her by telling her how angry Joe and I had been and how the anger would go away. She didn't really believe it then, but it made her feel better to know she wasn't alone in feeling such rage. The next day she started to come in each day to sit beside him for a while, just to touch him and talk about nothing very much or nothing at all.

"The anger was healed," she told me, "just by being with Aldie. He took it away. I don't know how. It wasn't anything he said. The reasons for it are all there, but the rage is gone."

# Second Plateau

TUESDAY MORNING after Christmas there was a dramatic change in Aldie's condition, a sudden deterioration which then stabilized into what I call the second plateau.

Until this time he had slept with his eyes and mouth closed, breathing fairly regularly. There had been increased swelling of the abdomen and though he was aware of the pressure, the paralysis saved him from acute discomfort or pain in that area. We had not yet instituted round-the-clock watches because I got my sleep when Aldie did and just woke people up if I needed extra hands. How I enjoyed those nights of the first plateau, alone with Aldie, sleeping while he dozed, rousing easily when he moved or needed something. The physiology of the 'crisis state' is truly remarkable. I was amazed at how well I felt, how rested, how alert, and yet how instantly I could sink into a dreamless sleep. People kept telling me to rest. I never could get them to understand that I was 'rested'. In theory I should have collapsed after it was over, but I never did. I simply started sleeping normally again. Obviously those two weeks – really three – required an incredible output of energy, but there was an incredible inflow that seemed to balance it out, leaving me with no physiological debit. Even as I was going through it, I knew that I was in some nonordinary state of consciousness. There was wonderful clarity, absolute confidence, and what I can only call a 'sense of flow'. Everything seemed to fit together perfectly.

Early on that Tuesday morning about five o'clock, Merdi,

Connie, and I had attended to a necessary cleaning up and bed change and, as often happened when there were night-time chores, we ended up at the counter drinking boullion before going back to bed. About six I settled down on my cot next to Aldie's bed, but found I could not sleep. As the dawn light began to gray the room I gradually became aware that something odd was happening. All the spaces in the room seemed to be coming alive with Aldie's presence —as if he were spreading out, filling up the air between my eyes and the ceiling, flowing all around me and into me, interpenetrating with me, filling up the spaces between the cells of my body. It was an indescribably warm, happy feeling. I remember looking up at the ceiling, which slants at an angle, and marveling at the palpable presence of him between it and me. I turned my head to look at the person on the bed beside me and reached out to touch his hand. There was the most peculiar sensation that the body beside me was irrelevant—as if Aldie were not really in it. Reaching to touch his hand seemed ridiculous when he was all around and through me! I lay there about an hour just enjoying it. About seven o'clock it seemed to fade and I fell asleep.

Waking at eight, I got up and went to stand beside Aldie's bed. With a shock I saw that a drastic change had occurred since we had tended him earlier that morning. He was sleeping with his eyes half open, and they were filmed over with gray. His mouth hung open and he was breathing in the pattern that the nurse had described. He did not re-spond to my movements as I dressed quickly, which was very different from other mornings. Believing the end was near, I woke the others and they came to stand in a circle round his bed—Jennifer, Connie, Merdi, and I. Matt stood a little way back in the doorway.

Aldie became aware of our presence. His eyes opened fully and lost the gray-filmed look. When he spoke it was with an entirely different voice. He was very much weaker, his enunciation was slurred, and each sentence cost him a great deal of effort. He glanced around the bed and knew immediately that we had sensed the change. The "wandering sportful soul"—a phrase borrowed from Montaigne years ago to describe himself—returned, and with it a remarkable twinkle in his eyes which had turned bright blue again.

"Well," he said slowly with careful effort, "let's celebrate!"

In our state of shock and uncertainty, this absolutely broke us up. The house rang with our laughter.

Then began the most incredible hour and a half. Aldie seemed to feel called upon to take center stage—a thing he had always avoided—holding it with such whimsy and humor that we could not believe we were hearing aright. There were exchanges with each of us, references to long-forgotten funny episodes. He was smiling in a way I had never seen before. Only much later did I realize with a shock what had made the difference. Aldie had very bad teeth, but no one, including me, ever really noticed because he had developed a way of smiling so his upper lip covered his teeth. Suddenly here he was smiling freely, letting all the stubby brown teeth show, and the effect was startlingly beautiful! That free, wondrous smile, combined with the spontaneous humor he was unfolding with costly effort, left us all helpless to do anything but respond with gaiety. We were too astonished even to take the initiative to see that he did not tire himself. Gathered in expectation of his imminent death, we were totally unprepared for what Merdi described in her journal that night as "the fragile unmasked humor, the unself-sacrificing humbleness, the sharp, beautiful changes in expression, and the ultimate reality of it all."

At last, after an hour and a half, he looked at me and said, "You girls must be tired. Why don't you go take a nap?"

I laughed and answered, "Are *you* tired?"

He nodded with a familiar impish grin, catching his lower lip with his teeth. And so we left him to rest, and

wandered the house like lost souls, unable to orient ourselves to this new development. Though there were occasional flashes of the impish humor again, this was the
last coherent exchange of such length, and the effects of
the sudden physical deterioration began to show. His abdomen, which had been slightly enlarged, began to swell to
immense proportions. We joked gently with him about his
pregnancy with 'mystical triplets'. His shoulders and arms
had gradually been losing flesh, but now they began to
appear shrunken and sharply skeletal. The right hand
which had pained him since August, a continual agony,
was held folded against his bony chest and curled there,
clawlike. His face hollowed, the domed forehead becoming
more prominent. His always regal nose (which had earned
him the childhood nickname "Beaky" from an irreverent
cousin) exaggerated the emaciation.

Sometime during the next two days he began to push
away the bedsheets and even the slit-back gowns we had
made him. Jennifer had brought him a long, softly woven
T-shirt with the words "Hot Damn!" stenciled across the
front. It was one of his most characteristic expressions,
and he had loved the T-shirt gown, but even that seemed
too confining now. Much of the time he needed to lie naked
although the temperature was chilly for Florida. We assumed he was experiencing fever, though his skin did not
feel hot. His coughing was getting much weaker and was
less and less effective in clearing his bronchial passages.
It seemed fairly certain that he would die of pneumonia
as his lungs were filling up. I was happy that we weren't
under pressure to "do" something about it. A phone conversation with Ken and a conference with the practical
nurse when she came the next day, made it clear that we
had come to the point where no one can predict the time.
Death could come at any time. Ken dropped out most of
the medications except for pain, and by the end of the
week we had stopped all medication in pill form as it had
become impossible for him to swallow them.

There was a strange feeling of anticlimax the day after the astonishing morning when we thought he was going to die. Merdi felt it too. Aldie sensed this and was so loving. He apologized for not dying! I held him close, wetting his pillow with my tears, and asked him to forgive me for the pressure of my expectations. When he went into his spaces there was something different. Often he would murmur "I don't know how," with a bewildered expression. It took me a while to stop feeling guilty and realize that he was into another place now where he had to struggle with something that was beyond my ill-timed expectations.

He frequently said things like, "It's time to go, time to go." I would tell him that he could go any time he wanted to. Once, he said, "I want to take you away from all this" (one of his favorite expressions), "but I can't find the door handle." He seemed to feel some confusion as to just how to do what next needed doing. It was very clear that he was experiencing his dying as something he had to *do*, not as something that was going to happen *to* him.

During the second plateau Aldie spent much more time in his spaces. His eyes never really closed again, even when he was resting. Most of the time his eyes were open but rather gray and distant, as if focused on things we could not see. They would still turn their deep bright blue when he came back from the spaces to focus on someone at the bedside, but it was obvious that it required a much greater effort than before.

People seemed to come by some sort of divine accident just as they were needed. The change in Aldie required closer attention on the part of the nursing staff and Suzie was a welcome addition. Suzie was a self-selected god-daughter who had lived with us for two years during a difficult adolescent time and had been very close ever since. She had planned to visit between Christmas and New Years. Aldie's dying did not deter her. We tucked her into a bed that is stored in the loft over the laundry alcove. My sister Marney and her close friend Charlotte came from

Honolulu the next day without burdening me with having to decide whether I wanted them or not. They just arrived and settled themselves into the same motel as Ed and Jane, whom they had never met. Marney and Char assumed roles in the household support crew, whose tasks were also increasing.

The weight of our experience was beginning to tell on Merdi and Connie and they both felt the need to have their Significant Other nearby—Clyde for Connie and Steve for Merdi. It seemed good to me that our daughters should share an experience, which was obviously changing them deeply, with the people who were going to live with the changes. I was also impressed by the courage of their two men, coming to meet a whole family for the first time under such crisis conditions. I knew it would be very easy to welcome with love these two new people into my life.

After the dramatic change in Aldie's condition, we decided we had better telephone Joe and Julie in Ireland and warn them that their January third flight, the first one they could get, might not get them here in time. It was a painful call for both of them.

While they had been away, Joey's anger, unleashed at Thanksgiving, had begun to recede and acceptance took its place. Joey knew Aldie was asking about him and that they must meet once more for their relationship to be fully resolved. Joe spent the few days between the phone call and the time they could get on the plane willing Aldie to live.

"He knew that I needed him one final time," Joe wrote later, "and equally that he needed me to let go, formally, while we were face to face with each other."

I believe Joey was right. Every day between the sudden change in Aldie on Tuesday and the Saturday noon when Joe and Julie walked into the house, Aldie would ask what time it was, what day it was, and when Joe and Julie would be there. Often he would look at me and ask, "Do you suppose Joey will be angry if I die?" I knew then that he would live until they got there, for no amount of assurances from me set his mind completely at rest. There was absolutely no question in anyone's mind that Aldie was waiting for Joe and Julie. The long period of stability after he had gotten to the stage where "death could come at any moment" was simply marking time.

It was characteristic of Aldie that he would be as motivated by others in his dying as in his living. He timed his dying to meet Joey's needs. Many people have noticed that dying people seem able to control the timing of their deaths — waiting for a holiday, or a birthday, or for someone to come, or someone to leave, or for someone to let go. Especially the last. During that second plateau it seemed so obvious that Aldie had to know that Joe and Julie could and would let him go. Everyone else had come the hard path to acceptance and Aldie knew it. He had had his final nothing-left-unsaid talk with Ric on the phone while he was still in the hospital and he had watched the rest of us come to acceptance as we cared for him. But he was not sure about Joey and so he had to wait — not just for Joey's sake, but for his own. There is a way in which the living can hold the dying back by not releasing them. A fully granted release — the laying aside of all angers, guilts, and needs — can be as great a gift as the gift of life. Who knows, perhaps it is a gift of Life!

Even though Julie was "reconciled to Aldie's dying," as she put it, the phone call and the realization that they might not make it back threw her into a state of shock. She was weeping on the phone. I tried to comfort her by telling her about my experience that Tuesday morning when I had felt Aldie's presence independently of his physical self. I suggested she go off somewhere alone, promising her that we would gather by Aldie's bed and simply concentrate on her with love. Afterwards, she wrote her version of that day:

> I fumbled my way to the door and headed out into the pitch dark. I was as upset as I had ever been from the begin-

ning of the cancer through everything. I was weeping and stumbling down the path that led toward the fields—wailing, I suppose they called it in the old days. Very suddenly a smile passed my face. It was as if someone else were in control of my face. And then a gush of joy flowed through my heart. Hey! I am thinking to myself, my good friend is dying and I want to cry and what is all this smiling stuff? And Aldie's voice said, "Hey, crazy kid in stateroom A!" [A private joke about Julie's bunk on the boat] Oh, Aldie, it's you, I thought. Oh, now I understand. You want me to be happy. There he is on his deathbed and he is still making jokes. Right then I began to heal. What was passing was okay. I could truly get into step with it. I sat down off the path near a gate and gazed up into the sky. The stars took me back to the sailboat and those incredibly close times of the night sails. Silhouetted against the sky was a gnarled old tree. I remember thinking at the time, I shall never forget the shape of that tree. That is Aldie's tree, and it will be a landmark for the rest of my life.

Later Julie called back with a message she had composed for Aldie that I was to read to him. It expressed her gratitude for "all that you transmitted to me through your humor, your dignity, and your patience." When I read what she had said to Aldie, he said in a sort of wondering tone,

"The darling! The darling! You have told me such wonderful things. I am deeply touched. Remarkable children! Remarkable child!"

"You have made them so," I told him with tears in my eyes. I finished Julie's message which ended with "I love you so." And Connie, who was standing at the other side of the bed, chimed in with, "You taught us how to love, Daddy."

Aldie looked up at me with genuine surprise and said, "I thought they taught me! I'm so happy!"

There was a rather childlike simplicity to much of what Aldie said during that last week that penetrated deeply. The two things that struck us all so forcibly toward the end were, first, the remarkable strength in his hands and arms and, second, the intimacy of his concentration upon each individual who came within his field of vision.

Many observers have noted the strength of grasp that dying people have, and Aldie was no exception. Not only did he grasp one's hand with determination, but he held us in his arms with a strength that was hard to believe, especially as his shoulders and right arm were the source of all of his pain. Often when I bent over him to nuzzle my face in its accustomed place between his shoulder and cheek, his arms would slip around me and hold me with all the male strength of our closest days. He held others, male and female, in the same way when they bent to kiss him. It was an incredibly intimate experience. Indeed, his capacity for intimacy was almost discomfitting for those new to it. When someone was beside his bed and he recalled himself from his spaces, his eyes became very large and dark, bright blue. They would fasten upon yours with such intensity that they seemed to bore past your mind, past any emotion, and into the very core of you. I know now what people mean when they say they feel uncomfortable in the presence of a truly holy man. Death makes all men briefly holy, if we let it. Such a look wipes out all pretense. There is nowhere to hide. It simply sweeps away anything that gets in the way of cleansing love.

Once near the very end, right after Joey had come, Aldie whispered to him, "Kiss me." Joey did, on the cheek, and Aldie said, "No, on the lips." And Joey did. They kissed a long moment and Joey said afterward that Aldie's lips were trembling. Then Aldie smiled at Joe — such a smile of love — and said, "Thank you." Our cultural training does not prepare us for the cleanliness and purity of total intimacy.

The force of the intimacy frightened Merdi a little at first. She kept a journal during the whole experience and wrote of the first day that she was here:

> With each of his children and each friend who drops in to see him he begins to remember things done together, reviewing them slowly as though his thoughts were linger-

ing there, seeing them afresh. He tells me how much he got from our friendship when I was young. He felt his dreams were reflected and caught fire in me – in our endless walks and whimsical talks that in my childhood daydreams seemed so real. He talks of how "it's so good to see that you can love another man besides me," and I see an intimacy that's frightening.

In her journal, she struggled with both the hope and the fear that Aldie's feelings for her were unique. Yet even as she wrote she realized that "love at its roots dissolves distinctions of kind and only if feared is it channeled into our twisted definitions of 'good' or 'evil'." Beautiful Merdi, writing out all the self-examination that death requires of us, allowing ancient jealousies and fears to be revealed and so to be resolved. A few days later she wrote:

> While sitting on the patio, cleaning the pebbles in the meditation pool, I finally realized what he's been saying to me about our "buddhood" when I was young. I finally felt it, deep and even, and it suddenly freed me of attachment of a certain kind to him. The freeing made me light, and I can let go my secretness of a special unique relationship with him which I was suddenly aware I had been harboring. Now I feel more able to include and be included with the rest. Very close and unique to him we each are.

Merdi was the only one who kept such an explicit record of her thoughts and feelings during the dying time. The rest of us wrote down our experiences after it was over. For me, the subjective experience was on such a different level of reality that I could not translate it daily into the logical processes that words require. Only later could I move back and forth between the two dimensions. We are grateful for Merdi's journal, for it documents certain interactions that may point to universals in the dying-grieving process.

The focus in a death is so much upon the dying person that one tends to forget the subtle dramas being played out between other members of the family. As our network tightened around its dying center, the qualities of each link became heightened, increasing the closeness, but at the same time exposing and exacerbating all of the tensions—some of them hidden since childhood. The shocking intimacy of a dying person's insight forces such revealings, even though they are never put into words.

Aldie had laid aside the burden of his ego and reached spaces where love surges beyond polite cultural limitations. There was a nakedness in the power and honesty of his love. While it carried all of us beyond our cultural inhibitions, it also uncovered some of the unlovely feelings that hide beneath those inhibitions. Our particular network holds great potential for tension between 'natural', 'adopted', and 'step' children; between 'kin' and 'non-kin' co-residents. For each family the content of these tensions would be different. It would be misleading to write of the incredible love that flowed through the family and the purity of Aldie's dying nature without showing how it exposed the very human impurities in those of us whose time to "lay aside the burden of ego" hadn't come yet. These tensions must be recognized and dealt with—but not necessarily through the conventional "talking it out." Death itself and the physical labor that a shared death requires, can be an even more effective solvent for guilts, jealousies, and angers. The journals and the memories that I asked each person in the network to share with me afterward record many of these tensions honestly, as well as the resolutions that came at levels far too deep to need words.

As Aldie became weaker, there was a tendency for everyone to want to be the special person he needed most, loved the best, or who could understand his mumbled words most clearly. All of us had to come to the point where we could experience our own uniqueness with and to him, and at the same time witness and respect every other equally unique relationship. The very close moments in life between family or network members usually occur separately, between two people or maybe three. Seldom do all of the significant people in a person's life express their most vulnerable, open moments with him under the eyes of all the others. We were forced to recognize the natural human jealousies and allow the divinity of Aldie's dying to heal them. When his articulation became very slurred and difficult to understand, I realized with a shock that Joey could understand what he was saying much better than I could. Even Connie, and then Suzie could pick up key words more accurately. I was jealous, plain and simple. But as the work went on, I realized that there were some things I was picking up in some entirely non-verbal way and also that my care for him was utterly dependent upon their better grasp of his verbal communication. The jealousy evaporated into gratitude.

There was a healing quality in the strange, nonverbal communication that several people experienced just sitting beside the bed while Aldie was in his spaces. Pat felt it as answers to unasked questions:

> As I sat with him, questions about death that I didn't know I had were being answered. It was just understandings, no rational information. And something was resolved about my father's death which happened years ago. I let go of a certain part of my father and a certain part of myself in a very peaceful way.

The healing came also through our repeated witnessing of the way Aldie related to each of us, even to friends or neighbors who dropped in briefly. There was such an intensity in his awareness of that particular person for that particular moment that those of us watching felt cut out. I remember especially how he gazed upon one neighbor—a good neighbor but not an intimate friend. He seemed to be searching for some incident in his memory that would be meaningful to that person and to no other, then he spoke the few words that called it up. This neighbor is not an unusually demonstrative person, but the directness and intimacy of Aldie's attention appeared to release something. Tears flowed uninhibitedly, dropping upon their clasped hands. I understood the tears. One weeps when one knows one's self to be wholly revealed and wholly accepted for a moment. It is like being forgiven—for nothing, for everything.

This happened with each of us—often within the hearing of others. There was a time when, sitting by his bed and holding his hand, I suddenly heard myself sobbing out the words, "Oh, Aldie I love you so much. I love you so much." I hadn't known that I would cry. It came unexpectedly after one of his long looks. I remember wondering if I were adding to his burden by weeping so deeply and so suddenly. But I saw the same thing happen with several others and I watched his face as they wept and I could see that their grief soothed his own. I could also see that each of them was absolutely, uniquely, and specially loved with the whole power of his being, yet it robbed his love for me not one whit.

# The Dialogue

THE LAST PHASE of Aldie's dying started the day before Joe and Julie were to arrive. The pain, which had been in abeyance since Christmas Day, returned suddenly and with great force.

Ever since the first diagnosis over a year before, Aldie and I had talked about and agreed upon some form of voluntary termination if the pain should become too intense. Just two days before the pain returned, we had looked at the various medications in my 'dispensary' and talked about what amount of each would be a lethal dose. Aldie was not familiar with some of them and suggested that I get a PDR (Physician's Desk Reference) to figure it out. The PDR is a weighty tome describing drugs in common use, their chemical constitution, normal dosage, specific physiological effects and side effects, and their potentiating or counteractive properties when used with certain other drugs. I had not found time to track one down before the resurgence of pain took Aldie beyond the capacity to discuss the problem.

With the pain came a change in his ability to communicate. It became even harder to understand him and he was so weak we had to lean right down next to him to hear. At the same time it became obvious that if we were going to use an overdose, it would have to be Demerol because the other drugs were in pill form and it would have been impossible for him to swallow them. I had started giving him

Demerol shots again as soon as the pain returned, but they were not very effective, even though I increased the dosage.

Both nurses were aware of the change, the practical nurse because it was her day to visit and the RN because she just happened to telephone to ask about Aldie that day. In almost the same words, both of them said, "Mrs. Hine, now don't you let him suffer!" I felt they supported me in using the medication according to Aldie's needs and not according to conventional amounts or time intervals. Yet I could not bring myself to ask either of them for advice about overdosing, nor would I have asked the doctor. It did not seem just to ask them to violate what I assumed to be their codes. Their support did give me the courage to give two shots much closer together than the prescribed three-hour interval. I have since learned that this is frequently done in hospitals with terminal patients and does not constitute unethical medical behavior. Nor did it constitute a lethal dose. But I did not know this then and was surprised at how much strength it took to give that injection. I found myself saying the Lord's Prayer out loud as I filled the syringe.

About three o'clock that Friday, Jennifer came out from the bedroom after taking a turn at Aldie's bedside and watching his pain. She challenged me in a voice full of tears, yet with an amazing strength in it.

"Mother," she said, "can't you kill him?"

The way she put it shocked me. I shall never forget her face. It was slightly twisted with still-furled sobs and there was anger and determination in it. Her eyes held mine demanding an answer. If I had not already known, I would have discovered it at that moment—our seventeen-year-old daughter was a strong and powerful woman.

I said simply, "Yes, I can" and told her that we had to figure out exactly what a lethal dose would be.

It could not have been more than half an hour later that a young couple, both medical students who have been dear to our hearts for several years, walked through the back door carrying a PDR! Then began what seemed, even at the time, an incredible comedy.

All those things you learn in college drama courses about the close relationship between comedy and tragedy really are true. The day had been a heavy one for all of us. The pain weighed upon us, grinding at our nerves. Even Claudia and Richard who had come early for the daily meditation felt the burden. The twelve or thirteen of us who were in the house at the time crowded around the counter, pouring over the PDR. Sections would be read aloud and discussed heatedly. The paragraph on the effect of Demerol on the respiratory system inspired detailed analyses of Aldie's breathing patterns, the amount of coughing, and speculation about just how full his lungs were. Ideas about overdosing in terms of amounts injected or the timing of a series of injections bounced back and forth across the coffee cups. Someone questioned the possible dangers of doing a 'half-assed' job. I do not re-member who was on watch in the bedroom, but it must have sounded like a mass uprising from in there, where I was certain Aldie knew what we were talking about. I felt sure he would be glad we had both the PDR and the input from our young medical students. Voices rose as the argu-ments became more detailed.

At one point, stepping back for a moment to survey the scene, I could not help but laugh. How incredible! Thir-teen people were yelling at the top of their lungs about committing what was supposed to be a crime. Such things were meant to be decided discreetly and happen quietly. While pooling our knowledge about drugs and physiology, someone suggested that the paralysis might be one of the reasons the shots I had already given were not as effective as they should have been. Along with the swelling of the abdomen, body fluids were beginning to collect in the lower torso. The edema was such that flesh bulged out from the hips, making it very easy to give injections without the painful turning and rolling. So it was decided that we would massage the area of the injection both before and after to assist circulation. I do not know if this actually made a difference, but we thought it did. By the time two more shots had been given, Aldie was beginning to get some pain relief.

As soon as the conference at the counter had come to a satisfying conclusion, I went right in to tell Aldie that I was now prepared to give him an overdose any time he wanted it. I'm sure he already knew. No extrasensory perception would have been needed to know what we had been discussing. He smiled and told me thank you, but that he did not want it right then. After that, every time I gave him an injection, I offered him the overdose if he chose — and every time he made the decision not to take it. Sometimes he would ask how long it had been since the last shot, and if it had not been long enough to satisfy him, he would refuse another. If he did not seem to be in great pain and the three hours had gone by, I would ask him if he wanted the shot. Sometimes he would say no. Between Friday and the time he died on Monday, my charts show a pattern.

Aldie had always been interested in biological and physiological rhythms. He had told me about studies showing that the same dose could be either therapeutic or lethal to experimental rats depending on the time of day it was administered. With Aldie a definite rhythm of need for pain relief developed. Late morning and early afternoon were the times he went without any at all. Aldie took control over the timing — and therefore the amount — of medication he was getting. He made a decision about the type as well.

I called the doctor on Saturday to tell him about the difficulty in getting complete pain relief. While the Demerol was more effective than it had been when we started it on Friday, Aldie was still restless and uncomfortable most of the time. The doctor suggested we switch to morphine.

Aldie's response to this was surprising. When I told him he became very agitated. His speech was very indistinct by this time and it was difficult to understand his words, but negatives and positives were still clear. He did NOT want morphine. Gradually we caught enough words for us to understand his reasons. It was important to him that he be able to rouse himself to communicate his experiences to us, and he did not want to feel 'blurry'. He was already engaged in a process that didn't become apparent to us until a few hours later. I think he was trying to tell me that the stronger sedative effects of morphine would interfere with an internal process he did not want to cut short. He seemed to be balancing the pain relief against his need for awareness to complete his task.

From that time on, Aldie's breathing became more labored. His mouth was always open and he was clearly suffering from the drying effects of it. He seemed grateful when I scrubbed gently at his teeth and gums with a wet washcloth. He was unable to drink from a straw, so we devised a way of dribbling small amounts of water or cold fruit juices into his parched mouth. We sucked up a strawfull, slipped a finger across the top of it, and released it over Aldie's tongue. The straw held just enough liquid to satisfy his need, but not enough to make him choke or cause difficulty in swallowing. I couldn't help wondering if the hospital alternative would have been a tube.

Connie's Clyde arrived Thursday and Merdi's Steve on Friday. Neither were part of the nursing team, but they took up their posts in a chair in the bedroom during the night watches when their respective beloveds were on duty. Sleeping on the cot next to Aldie's bed, I could see them as they watched and listened. Again I was glad they were there. How ever could Connie and Merdi have shared in words the experiences they were having? Steve, a very competent and sensitive person who has taught courses in death and dying, watched this dying with awe and humility. Though he had never known the rest of the family before, he is now part of all of us because of the valley we walked through together. This cannot help but have an effect upon his relationship with Merdi.

Clyde was the one with the wisdom to spell out the difference between those newcomers who should be on the nursing staff and those who should join the household support group. He had been called on to take a watch his second night while I rested, half-awake on my cot. The next day he said that he thought it had not been quite right, for him or for Aldie, and that the nursing staff should be only those who had known Aldie a long time and had lived intimately with him. Consequently, Clyde reassigned himself and began to chop wood for the fire and to transform our neglected jungle of a yard into the ordered beauty that met the eyes of those who came to the memorial meditation a week later. I was glad he helped clarify the roles, but I am also glad that he was called upon to take that watch, uncomfortable as it was for him. For something passed between Clyde and Aldie that night, which I saw through sleep-dimmed eyes, but did not really understand. Months later Clyde was able to write to me about that moment and about the emotions that gripped him, an outsider, coming into what he called the "aura of magic enthusing the house and its occupants":

When I first entered the room where Aldie lay, I saw him as old, not the robust captain I was somehow expecting. I grew angry and afraid. Angry because I didn't know him, never cared to know him, and circumstances never introduced us until so late. My rage made me fearful. I knew in my head that this was no place for anger and that it was some manifestation of hubric pride, but there I was, angry and unable to free myself.

Connie and I were on Aldie's right. As she bent to his ear, comforting and informing him of who I was, I moved to his left and into his vision. (Whenever I was with Aldie, he gazed up and to the left.) Hovering over him I felt myself a vulture about to live off the flesh of a once mighty bull, now open to my insignificance. He was in pain, dying and immobilized and I feared him—not the swollen belly, shrunken arms or gaunt face. What scared me was all that Aldie was, gazing from behind foggy, unemotional eyes.

I said, "Pleased to meet you," and kissed his cheek. He winced in pain, whether from the physical touch to his sensitive skin or from my emotional chaos inflicted on his bared psyche, I know not. At the time I believed the latter. Shortly thereafter I left the room and the powerful spirit behind me, and exchanged formalities with the people in the kitchen. Feeling I had stepped into an abyss, I heard the lines from Joyce's *Araby*, "Gazing into the darkness, my eyes burned with anguish and anger."

This first audience with Aldie set a tone of conflict. The major conflict I felt was the need to reverse the energy flow from the position I felt myself in, as alien and parasitic to Aldie, to a situation where I could be of support. On the second day I was there, Ginny, you read me clearly by saying to me that "the only sin in this house is to feel like an outsider."

During that night watch with Aldie, I found I could detach myself from ego's demands for worth and simply sit beside him, never talking to him or moving except to drip some water into his mouth when he seemed to want some. Once I watched his eyes clear and he spoke, not to me, but up and to the left. He put out his arm like a traffic cop saying, "Stop." He did something that night that resolved my insider-outsider, support-hindrance conflict. I thought he wanted some water and was about to give him some when his eyes opened *so* wide and he looked right at me. His lips were moving and I bent closer to hear what he was saying. He put his arm around me and pulled my cheek to his lips and held me there. I began to pull away but he really had me. He was strong. We seemed frozen with his lips on my cheek. I felt his presence soothing me with serenity. He showed me that he was so far beyond my petty feelings of inadequacy, so far beyond any innocent harm I could do him. He just held me to his lips emanating "no problem, no conflict, no pain, everything between us is as it should be, as it is, OK." He then released me. His eyes glazed again, he turned his head back to the left and slept. He seemed to float above the bed and glow.

I sat the rest of the watch wallowing in the peace of his presence. Aldie was not an old man who was dying, but an impeccable warrior preparing to lunge at Death, grab Him and ride Him into the wind. After that night I entered into a realm of meaning and purpose. I chop wood, do nothing, think nothing. I chop wood, do everything, and understand. The sky agrees, the wind agrees. Aldie grows weaker, dying. A warrior solidifies, eyes clearing, preparing. Everything is as it is, OK.

It was inevitable that Clyde and Steve should experience themselves as outsiders, yet it seemed fitting to me that there be someone to fill that role. Aldie and I had always had 'outsiders' around, weaving their once-removed kind of love in and around the live-together family members. For so many, like Claudia and Richard, the line between outsider and non-kin family member became so fine as to disappear entirely. (Indeed, since Aldie's death, Jennifer and I joined forces with them as co-residents and experienced no dislocation or period of 'adjustment' at all.)

Thus it was that when Joe and Julie finally arrived, they walked onto a crowded stage. It was a crucial moment in Aldie's dying. I remember weeping with relief when they came, knowing it would then be quick for Aldie. Joey wrote how it seemed to him when he walked in the door after thirty-six sleepless hours of travel:

> I remember seeing a blur of faces, none of which I can recall, in the kitchen and around the counter. I remember standing there, waiting in that sea of death. It pulled with inexorable strength at my strength. It was there for me to ford before I could enter 'his room'. My Rubicon, my irrevocable step into the future. All that had been my life was ending as I stood there. My adulthood was taking its first deep scar. And I was weary, so weary before it began. I remember feeling that I was at military attention, my back straight, my eyes on the crack in the closed door. They were tending to his needs when we arrived. It was a final act, that being kept waiting, that preparation.
>
> I saw Jennifer first. She stepped out of the room and off to one side and beckoned us, a motion that Mom immediately seconded. I looked from face to face of the women who had been with him—Suzie, whom I had yet to meet, and Merdi whom I had met just once, and Mom and Jennifer who did not watch us and yet watched our movement

toward the room. It took more courage than I had imagined possible. I had not thought of courage at all, but when it came time to move, those steps, those mechanical steps, were horribly difficult. It was so lonely a walk that I do not even remember being next to Julie or how I managed it at all. With every step I wanted to turn away, to say no, wait a minute, let me think, everyone leave the house, let me see him alone. I felt naked, watched by people who had never seen me before.

And then we were in there and I was saying something like, "Hello, old man. I'm glad to be home. Thank you for waiting." Even now — the thought of those words, of looking into his eyes, being held by them, within them, saved for a moment longer from looking at the ravages the cancer had caused — even now I want to cry — not for what happened later, but for that final goodbye which he and I had at that moment. It was the end of our relationship as equals, as close friends. From that moment on he would be ill and I would be healthy. He would be dying and I could do nothing to alter that. But for a moment we were as we had been and I looked and looked, silently taking all that I could of him, wanting to have forever imprinted that clarity of his person which rested for me in those eyes. The eye of the hawk. He had it. I knew he had it and so did he. Then it was gone and I was aware of those people all over the steps into the living room — those people who had been with him when I hadn't. Those people I didn't know and who were watching me act out this last scene with him.

I don't know how I stopped myself from hurling invectives at them, from saying, "Go away! For Christ's sake go away!" Then that too was gone and I was there. I was in Miami and Aldie was dying and I had no more anger toward anyone and I simply wanted to be near him for a while, to feel his person, to find out where he was, and see how much of him was left and how much had yet to be consumed by death.

In one way or another, each person had his final moment with Aldie, knowing that it was their special goodbye. And each, in his own way, gave Aldie the gift of release. Aldie had had to wait for Joey's gift, and then, receiving it, went into the final energetic act of his victorious dying — lifting from Joey the burden of anger. Months later Julie wrote:

When I walked into that room that day, I felt an electric charge go through my body. My heart stopped. His physical condition was so deteriorated. I had not known what to expect. I had never seen anyone that ill. But it was only for a second. Life flooded back into my body as I touched him. I was very much at peace, unable to make words or thoughts flow. I felt as if my offering to Aldie was Joe. I shall never forget the looks of the two men that day. Joe was more handsome than I had ever seen him—he radiated beauty. I was glad Joe looked so happy so that Aldie could see that Joe was at peace. Somewhere between Ireland and Miami Joe had found peace to bring to Aldie. Aldie's death has had an incredible effect upon our marriage. Joe's terrible, terrible anger is gone.

It was early that evening that the dialogue began. I did not understand it at first. Aldie had started to talk soon after his last exchange with Joey. He talked incessantly, unintelligibly, restlessly, almost energetically. And I could not understand him! At last, weary, I laid my head next to his and told him I was sorry I was not able to understand. He waved his left hand vaguely as if to brush something aside. I went out into the living room where a fire was lighting the cold night and wept on Richard's shoulder —helplessly.

Joey was on watch with Aldie and Connie was coming on next. At the time of the shift, Joey told Connie that Aldie wasn't talking to us, and told her to just listen without trying to respond. By the time I had collected myself sufficiently to go back into the bedroom, Connie and Joey had such stories to tell as lifted the burden from my heart. He wasn't talking to me! I wasn't failing him.

I began to listen with different ears. It was true. His eyes, distant and gray-filmed, yet somehow full of purpose, were searching the ceiling over my head as I stood at the foot of his bed. They were not sweeping aimlessly back and forth. He would focus now here, now there, on what appeared to us to be empty space. Sometimes it was as if he were talking to someone who was pacing back and forth. There were statements and questions, affirmations, and head-shakings. Some of what he said was understandable if your ear was sharp. Joey was best at understanding, Connie next best. I understood his words the least of anyone, except when he was answering a question of mine about his needs. Then I understood easily what he wanted. Those times were few in the last two days. Only infrequently did he pause during those two days and two nights to communicate his practical needs—or even to rest for very long at a time.

He was engaged in an exchange that seemed to have the urgency of decision about it. He was still able to amuse us briefly with a whimsy or an unexpected joke, but for the most part he was *working*. There is just no other word for it. Working at something, resolving something—all through a dialogue with someone or something we could not see.

Early that first evening, Joey had asked him if there were someone in the room with them and Aldie had nodded.

"Who is it?" Joey asked.

"Death," Aldie answered.

"What is death like?"

"Benevolent."

"Aldie, can you see God?"

A sly grin and a slow nodding, "Yes."

"Where is God?"

"Right behind death."

We came to accept Aldie's awareness of his death as a presence in the room. It wasn't weird, or spooky because there was no sense of death with a capital "D". Those of us who went through the experience with Aldie have a strong feeling for the specificity of death. There is no such thing as Death. There was Aldie's death, and there is my death and there is your death. Process? Presence? Person? Event? Whatever we call it, it is something special to each of us to be reckoned with, related to, perhaps lived with all along—respected, of course, but not feared. I had the feeling that Aldie's death respected him as much as Aldie respected death.

Another time when Connie was on watch, Aldie was alternately talking and listening, and Connie asked,

"Is he here?"

"Which one?"

"Are there two?"

A slow nodding.

"Who is the second one?"

"Love. Go get mother. I have to give her some."

Connie came to get me and told me of the exchange. I came to stand beside the bed and he looked down at his hands, folded, claw-like, on his chest. Slowly he formed them into a sort of cupped position that reminded me of receiving the wafer at the communion rail all those years ago when we still went to church. He raised his hands toward me as if to give me something very precious.

The problem of 'not knowing how' which had seemed to so bother him before, seemed resolved during the dialogue. He turned to Suzie once with his impish grin and said,

"I know how they do it now."

"Oh? How?"

"They just send down a little basket and you jump into it and then they—whisk it away!"—a wave of his hand!

Sometimes during the dialogue there was a sense of argument. Aldie would nod thoughtfully or say "yes" or "no," then speak with the inflection of a question, and appear to ponder the answer. Sometimes there seemed to be the energy of a crucial struggle. There was a triangular bar hanging over his head so he could raise his arms and grasp it, shifting his shoulders slightly against the bed. Once I watched as he grasped one end of it slowly in his left hand, turned it upright like a club and shook it slowly three times at the unseen presence. A victorious smile spread across his face. Later he turned to Connie who was beside the bed and said, "I'm winning. How about that?"

Frequently he would pantomime holding a cigarette, examining it closely, and then grinding it out slowly and forcefully in an ashtray. It seemed to be important, but none of us really understood. I wonder sometimes whether the struggles we seemed to be witnessing had to do with resolving the unfinished business of his inner conflicts. Cigarettes had always been a symbol to him of something he considered both a blessing and a curse in his own nature. He smoked two to three packs a day until the cancer diagnosis, and then again as soon as it was clear that the dying had begun. All our life together he had considered this a symbol of the undisciplined side of himself which threatened the fine-tuning our love required, and which kept him from the use of his potential. But it was also a symbol of his capacity for free, creative fantasy—his "wandering sportful soul" which had led us on wondrous journeys, geographically to exotic corners of the world and spiritually into new ways of thought and feeling. I used to watch this repeated pantomime as he was dying, wondering if in the alchemy of his death he was alloying the blessings and the curses, the goods and the evils, resolving their duality.

During one of those times he was talking completely unintelligibly, I was suddenly struck with the memory of the meditation he had had in October when he had seen himself in a struggle between life and death using two different languages, one unintelligible. Even though it was difficult to understand his speech, there was a distinct difference between his slurred and badly articulated English and the other utterances he made. Once, when Merdi was on watch, she asked him if he had, even then, a choice between life and death. She said he paused briefly in his preoccupation with the dialogue and said, "Yes." She asked him if he could decide to live.

"Yes—but it would involve a tremendous inner struggle."

"Are you involved in that struggle now?"

"Yes."

At that moment, outside in the living room where Steve and Clyde were playing the guitar and banjo, the music was getting louder and louder. It was bluegrass – Aldie's favorite. Aldie turned his eyes to Merdi.

"You like banjo music, don't you Aldie?"

"Yes, I love it."

She noticed that he was becoming more and more restless.

"Is it hard to listen to the music?"

"Yes!" he answered with a burst of the tension she had seen building. "I've got to get up! I've got to stand!"

"Would you like me to ask them to stop?"

"Yes," he answered with frustration and relief.

There were other times when he seemed to experience frustration or confusion at being recalled into our world. Sometimes the ring of the telephone, an unexpected household noise, or even someone asking if he wanted water, seemed to cut across the rhythms of the dialogue – causing him to start, turn his head, and frown as if confused or bothered by the interruption. Often, agitated, he would ask to get up or stand up, but when we tried to move him upright in the bed or swing his legs, the pain would stop him. It was as if these evidences of external life exerted a pull on him toward life that disturbed the balance of the inner struggle, drawing him back toward movement he could no longer make. In a life-and-death struggle, we always assume that the struggle is *for* life *against* death. The Pebble People network and all of our own heroic efforts had been a battle for Aldie's life. There comes a time in each human life when life itself becomes the lesser state and the victorious must struggle *for* death.

There must have been moments of great peace for Aldie during the struggle. Once when I was asking him about the presences he talked to he said, "Come here, I'll show you." I put my face down on the pillow next to his and twisted my neck around so as to be looking up at the places where his eyes were focused. We were quiet together there for a long time. Joey and Suzie, who were watching, said afterward that a stillness came over us both, and that finally Aldie asked with a smile, "How did you like it?" I don't remember that question. There is a blank place in my consciousness where those moments belong, as if I had been removed from my life temporarily but completely. I remember at the beginning looking at a particular place in the ceiling and being sorry that I wasn't seeing what Aldie was, and then it began not to matter. After that there is a blank until I straightened up again feeling just—quiet.

Odd things happen to time when you are living in two kinds of reality. One of the resentments I felt earlier was being cheated of an old age with Aldie. I had never been able to envision our old-age life together, but I had a picture in my mind of what Aldie would look like as an old man. It occurred to me with a shock one day that Aldie looked like an old man. Disease had done quickly what life would have done more slowly. At that moment I realized I had not been cheated of old age with Aldie. I was having it, and it was an utterly absorbing, remarkable experience. Thirty years were simply being telescoped into three weeks, and I was content. I understood perfectly, then, that there is no difference between thirty years and three weeks. It is difficult to remember that now, but when I can, the contentment returns—briefly.

During those last two days a most remarkable perception-warp took hold of all of us. I had begun to see what I can only call a Christ-likeness about Aldie's body. It had nothing to do with the emaciated figures hanging on sculptors' crosses. Nor was it the golden-haired image of Sunday school posters. It was just a Christ-likeness. I would stand at the foot of the bed and gaze upon the distorted body—the distended belly, the shrunken arms and knobby shoulders, the gray-filmed half-closed eyes and open mouth rimmed with yellow slime that had to be swabbed out several times a day. I would consciously focus my objective, rational, scientist mind on these travesties of my beloved's body and *see* the ugliness. But it would only last a minute. Then, again, I was seeing the beauty of Christ shrouding him like an aura. I said nothing to the others, for I assumed it was the imaginings of my overloaded brain. The others, who were seeing it too, must have felt the same way for I don't remember anyone mentioning it until Charlotte, my sister's buoyant friend, announced unashamedly that she would bring her camera the next day to get a picture of Christ! I don't know why the rest of us felt we had to dissuade her. We did think the flash would startle Aldie and she agreed, but I think we had other reasons too—discovering that the others saw what we did, we felt somehow tender of our strange perception.

The shared perception-warp involving the smell continued. The smell increased in intensity toward the end and continued to be perceived by us as sweet and pleasurable. Even Steve, so recent a newcomer to our folie-à-deux-for-eighteen, wrote in his journal:

> His tired, bloated, surrendering body seems translucent. There is an aura about him that does not suggest age or disintegration. It is a newness, a fresh reality that copies the ashen outlines of death and renders up the smell of roses and acacia.

The dialogue ended about two hours before his death. On the morning of the day Aldie died, we heard him say several different times, "Yes, I'm ready. Okay. Yes." Or "I'm so glad. I'm ready." He was addressing the presences he had called Death and Love, confirming and acknowledging as if an agreement had been reached.

# The Release

ON THE MORNING of Aldie's death, the RN, whom we'd all come to love, sat at her desk pondering whether or not to come this day as scheduled because she knew somehow that if she did Aldie would die. How could she know that we would be grateful for her presence?

The dialogue had ceased that morning about eleven o'clock and Aldie had gone into a long period of quiet. He was pulling at each breath and they were very shallow. The nurse came to the door about 1:30 PM and I walked with her into the room. It was time for a Demerol shot and I leaned down to ask if he wanted it. For the first time he did not respond.

The nurse suggested I get it anyway and I had just gone into my dressing room where I kept the medications when she said, "Mrs. Hine, you'd better come back." It was Suzie's watch and she and Jennifer were at the foot of the bed. The nurse went to get the others. Within moments the bed was ringed with everyone who was within call— Jennifer, Connie, Joe, Julie, Merdi, Clyde, Suzie, Pat. I stood at the head on Aldie's left with the nurse beside me and Jennifer across from me on Aldie's right. We watched as he tried to draw in a final breath, but no air would come. His shoulders rose and his face twisted briefly in the effort, and then relaxed. Complete stillness.

I said, "He's gone."

The nurse said, "Not yet. His heart still beats." She listened for a moment with her stethoscope and then said,

"Now." She stepped back, letting the family circle close.

Joey said, "It's twenty minutes to two."

I bent over Aldie to hold him, to press my face next to his, to speak the words I needed to say. I knew he was there, watching from the space above us. But it was the body I had loved so much that I needed to hold and speak to. Then I straightened up and Jennifer embraced him, whispering her words of love. She stepped away to make room for Connie, and one by one each person moved to the head of the bed opposite me and held him or touched his hand and spoke as they felt moved.

It was not a heavy time. Nor had the fullness of the release lifted us as yet. That came later. We simply stood there, after saying our goodbyes to the body Aldie had lived in. I noticed his wedding ring and said, "Oh! What should I do about his ring? Should it go with him to be cremated?" With wry humor the nurse suggested that it might not get to the crematorium and why didn't I save it. So I wriggled it off his finger wondering who I would save it for. For safekeeping I put it on my own finger under my wedding ring. As it slipped into place, I thought, "Oh! I've just gotten married again! I have just started into a whole new kind of love." So exciting and so powerful was this image that Connie and I went out two days later to buy me a 'wedding dress' to conduct the memorial meditation in!

I then closed his eyes by gently pushing the eyelids down. They stayed down pretty well. We discussed whether or not we should try to close his mouth, but someone reminded us that that would require tying his chin up with a cloth and some one else said he would look like he had a toothache. Finally we all agreed that since the mortuary people would be coming in a few hours, he should just lie as we were all used to seeing him, with his mouth open.

The next decision had to do with what he should wear to be cremated in and we unanimously agreed that it should be his "Hot Damn!" T-shirt that Jennifer had bought. So we slipped his arms into the T-shirt and I laid his hands on his chest in the way he had held them so often during the last two weeks. We lowered the head of the bed a little to make him look more comfortable.

Then followed one of the most remarkable times of the whole experience. The others started drifting away by ones and twos. Some were in the kitchen making coffee. Others wept quietly together here and there. Jennifer went into her room and changed into black tights. Putting one of Aldie's favorite Mozart clarinet concertos on the stereo, she turned the music up very loud and began to dance. I stood by Aldie's bed, looking out into the living room, watching her and I thought it was the most beautiful thing I had ever seen. At one point I noticed Merdi also watching her, and we smiled at each other across the space where Jennifer's lovely young body was swaying and turning.

Someone called Ed and Jane at their motel, and someone else called Richard at work. He left immediately and went to pick up Claudia but couldn't find her. So he had to leave a note telling her that Aldie had died and that she should come right over. He said he tried to find the right words that wouldn't hurt her when she read them. He crumpled up several pieces of paper before he finally left one with the words: "Aldie Soars!"

It became the family cry and how we loved Richard for his gift. Later that afternoon, Connie lettered a beautiful sign with those words encircled in roses which we put outside the front door to greet anyone who came.

The rest of the afternoon is a blur in my memory. There were telegrams to be sent, of course. The wording came easily.

"Aldie is free. Died Monday peacefully. Last words, I'm ready. Memorial meditation five PM Friday at home. Gathered family smiling and strong."

Connie and Merdi saw to sending them off. There was a friend at the newspaper to call, and the doctor, and the mortuary, to tell them to come. We decided four o'clock.

I can remember being beside Aldie much of the time, touching him, remembering, whispering to him. Others came to be with him too. People flowed, and there was such love. Joey went for a walk and kept saying, "Hello, Aldie," to the sky. He said the sky that day was "huge, open, and drawing away from the earth, bright and rich with life," and that children stopped their play to stare at a man talking to the sky.

Merdi's experience of that afternoon is recorded in her journal:

> I had been sitting at the counter. We were each in different clusters quietly around the house. I watched the nurse, whom I like so much, move up to Aldie's room with Ginnie, and went back to my coffee. Then the nurse drifted smoothly over and said it was time—to come. Already most of the others had slipped into the room and stood peacefully around the bed.
>
> Ginnie's face was radiant, intense, smooth. I felt no anxiety or even a jolt. It was part as all the other parts had been—this one surprisingly easier. We'd been told to expect a death rattle—but as I stood with my arm around Connie I saw a man who'd taken his last breath and was pulling in, in, for another. No pain. No anguish. A reflex, then it all stopped. I watched with mixed curiosity. I'd never seen a dead person. I kept expecting to see his chest rise. We asked the nurse things like how to close the eyes. We laughed at our blundering questions—of what to do with a man who was dead, what the procedure was.
>
> There was a mixture of relief, joy, tender sadness, and uncertainty of quite how to react. Blundering together, we touched each other, and him who we felt was very much there.
>
> We left him in his room, the double doors wide open to the living room. Each of us wander in at our own time and touch him, kiss him, talk to him, sit in the chair beside the bed and laugh or cry or vacantly look out the window.
>
> The house is caught up in a swirl of peaceful and mad activity.

Steven wrote a song while Aldie was dying and I find it very beautiful. He described the writing of the song in his journal:

Early in the afternoon, I went outside with my banjo and sat in the dying man's car. I smoked part of a joint and got depressed. I thought about Meredith, about a gift I could give her, something lasting. I tried to write a song to her father. Nothing came. I played an old tune I had composed. It needed a refrain melody. I tried to make one. Nothing came.

Then, abruptly, there was a change. My mind ceased to spin its wheels. I closed my eyes and was back in the boat shed in Canada, on the bay. It was early morning and the tide was full and silent as glass. As I looked out at the boat riding at anchor, I saw a kingfisher dive from the mast into the water, falling so awkwardly graceful. Two goldeneye ducks, perfect jewels, were feeding – disappearing and reappearing without a splash. The circles outgrowing from their merging and emerging pulsated, converged, and intersected in a pattern, precise and beautiful.

And then the words came all at once in a rush, to the tune I had been playing. I could hardly contain my pen. It scrambled across the page of its own accord. I started crying. What was coming out was a song to the dying man, and as the words appeared fresh, so did sensations of inexhaustibility. Then came the refrain, easily, sliding, relaxed, into major chording, simple and effective. In ten minutes it was done, except for the last line. At this point Clyde came out from the house looking for me. He said, "You'd better get in there. The time has come." I closed my journal and hurried to the bedroom where the entire family was grouped around the bed. They were smiling and laughing about a T-shirt they had put on him. It said "Hot Damn!" in shocking pink letters. The man was dead. He died a few minutes ago Ginnie said. I burst out crying. Later, I added the last line to the refrain.

*Goldeneye*

Fisher king
mast-high
you dive into the sky.

How perfectly
you fall
till falling is all.

The waters
wide and deep;
we dreamed you fell asleep.

O sailor
in the wind
Your journey begins.

    Reach up to the sun,
    Your life has just begun,
    Your children left behind
    As the miles unwind.

Nowhere
is abiding —
where are you hiding?

Goldeneye
you're gone
southward like a song.

The angel
at your side
has opened the tide,

And wings bright
as the light
beat against the night.

    So fly, Goldeneye,
    Until you pierce the sky.
    The arrow of your breath
    Is not aimed at death.

 

Promptly at four o'clock the smooth-rolling black hearse arrived. The sight of it caught at my heart for it was so clearly out of place, and it meant that the final stages of Aldie's return to the sea and the sky would happen somewhere else. I pushed the thoughts out of my mind and reminded myself that Aldie was no longer imprisoned in that body, so why should my thoughts be. The two men who, quite unjustly, have been referred to ever since as 'the ghouls', came to the door and the marvelous comedy of it all swept over me.

I remember enjoying the feeling of welcoming them graciously into the living room where they perched sedately upon chairs. One was unctious, the other gaunt. Poor men! How insensitive, how irreverent we must have seemed to them. Smiling and relaxed, Joey and I sat with them, giving them the information they needed to fill out their forms. While they struggled desperately to keep the exchange in conventional channels, we kept asking them what we thought were pleasant questions about what happens to gold fillings and if they melt or should we pan the ashes for gold. We weren't really trying to upset them. It was just that there was no weight to our thoughts to keep them from flying into any corner of curiosity. And we were curious! We wanted to know! If something occurred to us to wonder about, we asked about it. We realized we were despoiling their solemnity unmercifully, but we could not squash ourselves into the proper feeling boxes.

Finally they rose and moved on their silent feet to get the stretcher from the hearse. They rolled it up the steps into Aldie's room and *closed the door* — shutting us firmly out. That seemed so terribly funny. After all we had been through with the rolling and the lifting and the bathing and the swabbing to have strangers protecting us from the indiscretions of that final move was just too much.

Richard, Claudia, and Merdi could tolerate it no longer. Indignant at what Merdi called "the impersonal and ridiculous way Aldie was being taken," the three of them went out in the yard and decorated the hearse with philodendron leaves and small white flowers that grace the weeds of our 'lawn'. When I saw the men wheeling the stretcher out to load it in the back of the hearse, my heart caught again and I followed them out the front door. I caught sight of the hearse in its jaunty dress and was just thinking, "Oh, how perfect!" as the two ghouls began snatching and ripping at the leaves and flowers, hurling them to the ground and almost stamping on them!

Surprised, I said to the unctious one, "What's the matter? Don't you believe in flowers?"

Human at last, he turned to me and said, "You wouldn't want me to lose my job, would you?" And of course, I wouldn't. Richard and Claudia and Merdi never forgave them, but I did. I felt really sorry for them, caught every day all day long in that web of impersonal dignity.

As I turned to go back into the house, there was the sudden lurch of knowing that Aldie's bed would be empty when I went back into the bedroom, and I realized that I could not possibly spend a night beside it. So I called the medical supplies rental place and asked them to come and get all of their equipment immediately. They couldn't do it on such short notice and so late in the afternoon, of course, but would come in the morning. So I asked whoever was standing next to me to take down the bed and store everything in the garage for pickup the next day. It seemed a crowd swooped down upon that room and within half an hour there was no trace of the hospital room it had been for two weeks.

We had not been able to contact Marney and Char as they were at the airport waiting to get a flight home. They were having lunch when Char suddenly paused, her fork in midair, and told Marney, "I can see Aldie with the family all around his bed. He's gone. We've got to get to a phone." They put off their flight till the next day and took a taxi back to the house, arriving just in time for the five o'clock meditation.

That afternoon, the meditation had a magic about it. Several of us had the same impressions of Aldie's presence in the sky and the gentle wind that was moving the trees as we sat out there by the pebble pool in our silence. There was a tremendous feeling of release, of joy, and such wide-reaching freedom. And yet Aldie seemed closer—closer than he had ever been, even in life.

After the meditation, Marney and Char decided we should have a proper wake and appointed themselves the 'booze committee'. They were the last of the group to come into the house after Aldie's death and they remember being struck with the sense of unity and joyousness. "Not happiness, but joy, as if everyone were letting go, unleashing." Everyone agreed to the idea of a wake and a most remarkable evening began.

It is probably significant that I have to depend entirely upon other's memories for this account. I have only very vague recollections of it, like images that drift in a mist. There were all kinds of music, and everyone danced at one time or another – each in his own way and to his own kind of music. I am told that someone dug out my collection of classical Hawaiian chants and that I did a hula, a dance form I studied forty years ago! At one point a particularly lively rhumba inspired a snake dance which involved everyone in a long line winding in and out of the living room and kitchen. We all sang – old time songs, children's songs, rock songs, country Western, religious songs. There was a lot of solo dancing with no one watching – just a private expression. Someone sent out for Chinese food and I am told I ate two plates full, my first 'real meal' in two weeks.

Marney and Char said there were times when everyone seemed to be talking at once but not to anyone in particular. They described it as "almost ceremonial, an unstructured ritual." Many, many times, and I do remember this, someone would say "I'll bet Aldie is enjoying this," or "This is what Aldie would have wanted." We were celebrating Aldie's release and our own, but strangely there was no sense of parting in the release. Aldie was very much alive and part of that exuberant evening.

The next day a few of us went to slosh through Aldie's and my favorite cypress slough in the Everglades. We listened to the wide silences, rested on fern-covered logs, and stared at the reflection of clouds racing across the still, clear water around our ankles. It is a beautiful place to take a big tuck in the distance between self and universe. Then we came back to the little rhythms of decisions that a death requires.

With a wisdom that came from somewhere deep within, I knew that there were some things that would have to change and be changed *fast*. One of them was the bed that Aldie and I had slept in all of our life together. I stayed on my little cot until two days later, by which time I had a new single bed and had arranged all of the furniture in the bedroom so that it looked different and required different space patterns to move through it.

Another thing that had to be done immediately was the disposal of Aldie's clothes and personal possessions, like shaving equipment. I told all of the men in the house that when Tip and Ric and Tim arrived for the memorial service, which was to be in four days, I expected them to divide up Aldie's things amongst themselves and have his closet and bureau drawers empty by the weekend. This included his watch and his billfold, which was curved to the shape of his right hip. Those two things used to lie on our bedside table every night and they were the most Aldie-ish things he owned.

That was one of the smartest decisions I ever made. Instead of weeping over them days or weeks later, trying to decide what to keep and who should get what, it was all done within the space of an hour or two in a furor of male laughter. Everyone got what he really wanted and I don't even know who has what.

I especially remember passing the doorway of our bedroom on the day of the memorial service, and watching Ric, who used to be just the right size to fit Aldie's J. Press suits but no longer was, fitting one of them on Peter with the eye of an experienced tailor. Peter and Joanne were two of the people who had lived with us for two years as an intimate part of our household but had never met our sons who live in Minnesota. It had been a somewhat strained meeting, the day of the service, and Ric's assignment of those suits to Peter threw a bridge across a peculiar gap in relationships.

The second day after Aldie died I remember because it was shopping-for-the-wedding-dress day. Connie and I picked out a handpainted white caftan for my 'wedding dress' and then extended the image that pleased us so much by including 'bridesmaid dresses' for her and Jennifer. The mood was one of celebration and excitement. The sense of release that started with Aldie's last breath seemed to be building toward the climax of the arrival of the rest of the family and the service itself.

I moved through that week after Aldie's death in a kind of protective bubble and was not aware until later of some of the tensions, adjustments, and pain that people around me were feeling. I think, though, that they were grateful that I was riding so high and so steady. It helped lift them over the danger spots as, later, they would each take their turns at lifting me.

It was inevitable that the adjustments between 'insiders' and 'outsiders' would have to be faced. This was complicated by the fact that there were two kinds of insiders — there were close kin as compared to non-kin, and then there were people who had shared the hard work of the dying as compared to those who came after the death. Many people had the problem of being an insider by one measure and an outsider by the other! Not one of us went through the soul-searing intimacy of that death without at least one total stranger at his side!

Each felt the tensions differently and for different reasons. Steven's journal reflects a deeper source of strain and is beautiful in its honesty:

> Meredith has been powerfully influenced by the events of the past week. She will never be the same again. It will be some time before we again share what we had before. The death of Aldie has not yet drawn us closer together. I feel estranged, but try not to show it.
>
> By the time I came, she had been with him for a week and a half, love-watching his metamorphosis with his wife and three sisters. I watched her looking ardently into his

eyes. Clearly she was hooked into the same circuit, the two of them sipping a rare wine brewed of memory and of blood. I felt excluded. I felt, suddenly, welling up from my viscera, an unreasoning jealousy. The fact that I was jealous, and of a dying man, enraged me, making me fear for my sanity. Almost I was ashamed that I was alive. It came as a shock to me to realize that, even in death, such emotions were present, arousable, and ready to possess the purest heart.

Joe and Julie, coming in at the end, felt understandable jealousy for those non-kin who had been with Aldie during days when they were prevented from being there by crowded airline schedules. There were really ridiculous incidents like the evening Joey was sitting in the living room staring into space, exhausted from a watch with Aldie, when Clyde came up to him and said, "I don't believe we've properly met," and put his arm around Joey and kissed him. For Joey, the feelings of antagonism for the people he considered 'outsiders' began to fade during the week after the death. He wrote:

> When I came I was harsh in my attitudes about these others and easily antagonized although I don't think anyone knew of my feelings. I considered it a family affair, much like Ric, Mol, and Tip felt when they came. Like them, I was not pleased with the presence of these interlopers. But that was a feeling I had only while Aldie lived. It kept me free of any need to include them in my thoughts, free of their presence, in fact. Once Aldie was gone, I was aware of the position I held as male 'host'. In that role I did come to know and appreciate Steven and Clyde, even more, to like them both and to love them in that special air of that time. Like warriors huddled in a trench, we will have common memories which transcend common feelings or traits. But I think it is going to take time, being near one another again, for us to be friends as I would have us be.

When the Minneapolis contingent arrived on Thursday, they felt the same shock at being confronted with so many 'interlopers' upon a 'family' event. Ric still refers to the situation that he walked into in this house as 'the zoo'. And yet they saw that without such an extended network which, by its nature included 'strangers', the work load of Aldie's death could not have been carried. It could be argued that if all of the outsiders had been replaced by blood kin we would have had about the same number of people to share the load. But I do not think this would have brought us to the experience that we had.

I truly believe that the strange mixture of relationships was part and parcel of the transforming death for us. I think that only those who, for one reason or another, were drawn to the experience should have been here. Who can say why certain people needed to be here and others did not? Or why Aldie needed certain people and not others at that time? Reason and logic and conventional concepts of family cannot carry us to such answers. The response to a particular person's death must come from the depths of one's own spiritual needs at the time and not be clouded with ideas of 'duty' and burdens assigned by accident of birth. People should participate in a dying because they need to, not because they think they ought to. I think people who are unafraid of death would know which dyings they ought to be part of and which not.

Tim, like Tip and Ric, knew he did not need to participate in the death, but that he belonged at the service. In a beautiful letter, written later, he explained some of his sensations upon entering 'the zoo' the day before the service. He also described, in his own special, brilliant style, an experience he had the day of Aldie's death.

> As soon as I stepped past the threshold into that dear, familiar home, I felt that I was as a fleck of bark swept into a stream which had steadily engorged itself. The direction and momentum was as pure and spontaneous as any river, and its surface, at the same time, as placid. There was a tireless current of vitality about the family (and it is so easy to speak collectively). I could detect a powerful union between the members, resulting from mutual participation in the awesome experience.
>
> I had chosen not to be present for the final days, a fact which, it seemed, many did not understand. They would

cautiously detour the conversation when it verged upon the subject of my absence, and this made me uneasy. To add to all the other contradictory sensations, I felt there was a conspicuousness about my presence because I had had no part in this colossal event. The others had weathered the tempest; I was but part of the eddying emotional gales which trailed the front.

I had had a wondrous experience the day of Aldie's death. When Joey called me early that afternoon, I was struck at once with the conviction that I must go to Mount Tamalpais. My stomach tingled and felt strangely hollow and light. There was not an instant of deliberation. I got in the car and followed the torturous bends I know so well. I parked on the ridge and walked off the road, scrambling up a pinnacle of granite, exposed and crumbling above the ravine. Grasses plummeted smoothly to the burnished wrinkles of the Pacific.

I was not alone. My vigil was accompanied by the wet blasts of fog, the pines in animate sway, the ocean, and Aldie. He was beside me; he enveloped me; he beckoned me. I could vent no grief. He was the mute voice inside of me that said, "Look! Look! This is our prosperity. I am now there, but so have you been all this time." I felt the earth. I watched the sun ooze into the horizon, and welcomed the infiltrating salve of darkness as it unveiled the infinite tract of the stars. I was privileged to the drama, and it seemed to me that Aldie had given me his last and most personal gift.

I drove that car back with the assurance that Aldie had unshouldered both the freight and the loves of his life for an existence far more tranquil than I could comprehend. I knew that he had in no way parted from his loved ones but is, instead, a part of what is all around us.

Could Tim have shared Aldie's release in this way had he been there? I doubt it. The transcendent quality of the experience was not limited to the people who witnessed the dying. For Tim, as for Tip and Ric and Molli, their time to come was the day before the service to help in the sharing that reached a wider circle.

Thursday night all planes had been met and twenty-four of us gathered around the fire to plan details for the next day. Tip, Ric, and Molli and the two grandchildren had come from Minneapolis. Tim had arrived from California, and Peter and Joanne were due in the next morning. I don't know where they were all bedded down. Some were in Claudia and Richard's apartment, some in sleeping bags in various nooks and crannies. A list of things that needed doing spilled itself out from my head onto a piece of paper, and other people added other items. The list was read as we sat around the fire, everyone picking the jobs that appealed to them — borrowing huge flower pots and filling them with gladiolas, icing the wine, arranging the cheese-and-crackers table, setting up the tape deck, directing the parking of cars, greeting people at the door. It all seemed very easy. Most of the major decisions had been made before. Aldie and I had talked about it and agreed that it was logical to simply elaborate on our usual five o'clock meditation time. Most of the people who would come knew why we had started it the year before, even though many had not been Pebble People. I could not imagine anyone else conducting a service about Aldie. No one knew him as well as I did nor could anyone speak for him with the authority I could. The words that I would use had been forming themselves in my mind all during the two weeks of his dying, weaving themselves out of things he said and things we experienced. And so it was easy to write the short, five minute statement I wanted to make before the usual fifteen minutes of silence.

# Memorial Meditation
## Friday, January 9, 1976, 5:00 PM

Before we join in our time of meditation today, there are a few thoughts I would like to share with you.

To those of you who have not been present at our five o'clock meditations during the past year, I would like to explain both our choice of setting and the informality of this memorial. Aldie did not live his life primarily out in the world of achievement. His center of gravity was in his home and in the people who shared it with him—whether family in the conventional sense or what we like to call our extended kin. Aldie did not live with much attention to structure and formality. What ritual there was in his life was mostly of his own making. Therefore it seemed fitting for us to come together to honor him in his own home and through a memorial ritual of our own creation.

Eight years ago when we moved into this house, Aldie and I wrote a prayer which we read together during a little homemade service of dedication. I would like to read part of that prayer now to welcome you all today in that same spirit:

"Almighty God, we ask that your Holy Spirit be present in this house now and henceforth. We ask that whatever we are motivated to do in your service, either within this house or out from it, will act upon us in such a way that we are drawn ever closer together through the 'wholing' quality of love.

"We recognize that there are forces too powerful for us to handle, which work to separate us from each other and from you. We commit ourselves and those who live here with us into your care for protection from these alienating forces.

"Bless those who are drawn, for whatever reason, to this house. And bless us as we receive them into it.

[154]

Grant us all the sensitivity to perceive the thoughts
and desires of each other's hearts. Grant us also the
power to participate in the redeeming, transforming
work of love in each other's lives.

"We ask that strength, joy, warmth, and loving
gratitude be continually renewed through the relationships that occur in this house, and we dedicate it
to you as a center for your holy love, to be used according to your purposes."

That was our commitment eight years ago. I would like to
renew that commitment now and to witness my conviction
that Aldie and I still work together in love even though we
do so from different energy levels.

We have gathered together today to express our love for
a beautiful person. There have been dark times behind us
and there will be dark times ahead. But today let us be joy-
ful in the completion and fulfillment of a unique life. It is
very human to experience the sense of outrage – the anger
and indeed the fear that such a death brings up in us. But
we who have been living closely with death in this house
for the past three weeks have discovered that death is wholly
compatible with life and joy. We have also found that death
is more of a process than an event. While it is certainly a
physiological process of deterioration, it is even more importantly a very beautiful transformation of consciousness.

We were able to control the physical pain with medication so that Aldie's mind was free for what seemed to
be a gradual transformation of awareness. Until the last
two or three hours he was able to communicate some of
what he was experiencing. His wonderful whimsical humor
threaded in and out of the process, causing this house to
be filled on occasion with most unseemly laughter!

He never spoke as a victim of death – but rather as someone in long and intensely personal dialogue with a presence
he described as "benevolent." Aldie appeared to have a
surprising amount of control over the process – certainly of
the timing. He spoke frequently about his lack of fear, and
talked about the peace and freedom of surrender. He made
a clear distinction between giving up and surrendering. He
talked a great deal about how happy he felt and how satisfying and fulfilling his life had been. There seemed to be no
sense whatsoever of regret that it was ending sooner than
might be expected. He seemed to have entered a space
where time was irrelevant.

A few months earlier Aldie had told me that he was very frightened of death – terrified of becoming physically helpless – afraid of the humiliation and indignity of the terminal stages of cancer. But as the reality came upon him, he said "When it happens you find out that all your fears are illusory – they don't mean a thing. The whole ego thing – it just disappears. It's nice to be free of that burden."

Aldie was deeply grateful to all of you who put so much energy into our healing network last year. He never believed that his dying would mean that we had failed. He felt that the reprieve it gave us and the continued fight had been necessary to the transformation that was even more important than life or death. A year ago, he said, he could not have met death without fear. There is a quotation from Laurens Van Der Post which has been a great comfort to me in the past weeks. It helped me understand why we all had to work so hard toward the hope for life and yet accept his impending death positively:

> Man is charged by life to do everything in his power to defeat death if only to make certain that when it ultimately comes it is the right kind of death, and that at the final transition he can achieve a transfiguration of anguish into utter peace of spirit.

Before we join in our fifteen minutes of meditation, will everyone please join hands with the people on either side of you to form a network linking all of us with each other in common love for Aldie. For one moment, let us all together transform our grief for him into a sense of union with him. Know that past and future are one – and that nothing can separate us from that love which flowed to us through the life of Alden Hine.

It was a beautiful experience and people stayed afterward to enjoy the wine and cheese we had prepared on the terrace and to share their love. Julie wrote about the service and the party to a friend two weeks later:

> Mother conducted the memorial service at home. We went out and bought the most beautiful dresses we could find. Mother wore a flowing white dress she called her wedding dress. She stood there and told the people what had happened to us, and they listened! They were all over the house, on the floor and on the tables. Some were confused at first, with their heads drooping. But she started

to talk and all their faces turned to her like flowers to the sun. She told them how we laughed, and things Aldie said. Join us in love and happiness, she said.

Jennifer wore a pale green satin dress covered in lace with sweet peas in her hair. She looked so beautiful. Aldie loved it—it was how he liked to see us.

The crowd! How we laughed after the party. I looked at Jennifer—her hair was dishevelled and she was looking kind of flakey. Then Connie staggered up. What happened, I said. We were mauled, they said. So was I, I said. Everyone was hugging and kissing me, people I've never seen before. My flowers are squashed. Aldie loved it all.

I never knew it could be like this, people said as they left. Man, neither did we, but it's great. Let's have a little more of this love!

I had been a bit concerned that people stay only for an appropriate amount of time. I felt, somehow, that an hour after the service would be about right and the men in the family were prepared to gentle people out if it went on too long. But it was not necessary. People stayed for exactly the right amount of time and started to melt away as if some celestial alarm had rung.

As I read the service that afternoon, I was aware that I was being considered 'strong' and 'brave' and having 'control' and all those other meaningless things. It wasn't that at all. My voice came out all strong and full because I felt strong and full inside. The words were comforting and helpful to people because they were born out of a joy and a release that was part of the experience. I knew this magnificent high would not last and that there were terrible, terrible times ahead. But I could see no reason not to maximize the joy while it was there, to spread it as far as it would reach, to touch as many hearts as possible with the incredible energy that had been generated.

This book has been written for the same reason. That, and to remind myself, now that I so desperately need to remember, that it happened just the way it did. I am stronger for remembering, and glad that one day it will be my time for the fulfillment of death.

# Afterword

*"You must needs leave so that*
*I may love you for your real being."*
Pir Vilayat Inayat Khan


The purpose of this book, when it was written a few months after Aldie's death, was simply to tell you and anyone else who wanted to listen, what a magnificent experience death can be. Now, writing this afterword from the vantage point of two years of lived-in grief, I can point to yet a third stage in the journey and an even more awesome discovery. I know now that death is truly the fulfillment of love. Before Aldie's acceptance of his death, while we were still fighting for his life, we were certain that our love required life for its expression. All through our life together we had known that love is the purpose of life, that life fulfills itself in love. What we did not know, and could not possibly have accepted, is that death is a necessary part of love. All who love must one day die. All lovers must, at some time, be stretched in grief across the ultimate chasm for which the little deaths that punctuate the course of deep love have only imperfectly prepared them. Only by experiencing this stretching have I come to know that bereavement is a necessary stage in the growth of love. As life fulfills itself in love, so love fulfills itself in death. To record the process through which one family came to know this truth in the deepest places of their souls is the final purpose of this book.